Advertising Annual2001

Advertising Annual2001

AdvertisingAnnual2001

The International Annual of Advertising
Das internationale Jahrbuch der Plakakunst
Le répertoire international de l'art de l'affiche

Creative Director: B. Martin Pedersen

Editor: Heinke Jenssen

Art Director: Lauren Slutsky

Editorial Assistant: Michael Porciello

Art & Production Assistant: Joseph T. Liotta

Published by Graphis Inc.

Dedicated to Gene Federico (1918-1999)

The International Annual of Advertising
Das internationale Jahrbuch der Plakakunst
Le répertoire international de l'art de l'affiche

Opposite: Fallon McElligott's "Hot Dog Umbrella" for Qualcomm

ContentsInhaltSommaire

Remarks: We extend our heartfelt thanks to contributors throughout the world who have made it possible to publish a wide and international spectrum of the best work in this field. Entry instructions for all Graphis books may be requested at www.graphis.com.

Anmerkungen: Unser Dank gilt den Einsendern aus aller Welt, die es uns ermöglicht haben, ein breites, internationales Spektrum der besten Arbeiten zu veröffentlichen. Teilnahmebedingungen für die Graphis-Bücher sind erhältlich unter: www.graphis.com.

Remerciements: Nous remercions les participants du monde entier qui ont rendu possible la publication de cet ouvrage offrant un panorama complet des meilleurs travaux. Les modalités d'inscription peuvent être obtenues auprès de www.graphis.com.

Opposite: Work for Kendall Jackson campaign as shown on pages 48-51

CommentaryKommentarCommentaire

Opposite: US/WebCKS's colorful ad for the iMac

Macintosh

DickCalderhead:
What If There Had Never Been A Stephen Jobs?

"The Fall of an American Icon"
Business Week
August, 1999

"There are no second acts in American lives."
Francis Scott Fitzgerald

"Apple's board of directors did the wrong thing when they allowed the Ghost of Christmas Past, Steve Jobs, to return. Letting this meddler loose in Apple at the most critical juncture in the company's history wasn't very smart."
Jim Seymour, PC Magazine critic
January, 1998

"Apple still has 'opportunity' written all over it. But you'd need to recruit God to get it done."
Charles Haggerty, CEO, Western Digital
August, 1997

"Bringing back Steve Jobs was a huge mistake. My advice is to…sell the pieces of Apple…for the best prices they can get"
Al "Chainsaw" Dunlop, Cashiered ex-CEO, Sunbeam
August, 1997

In 1997, they were ready to pull the sheet up over Apple. "They" being the corporate suits, the marketers, and especially the media. Most notably, *Business Week*, with it's cover story. Not so fast. From the shards of corporate disaster, which is where Apple was without Steve Jobs, Apple has once again emerged a vibrant, innovative company. *And the iMac is once again the most popular individual computer in America*. While investors and "corporate strategists" were all set to carve up Apple and sell off its assets for whatever they could get, Steve Jobs saw things differently. He knew the secret of saving Apple was what made it great in the first place: Innovation. No wonder Steve Jobs is held in such high regard by creative people everywhere throughout the graphics world.

When you think of all the truly innovative breakthroughs Steve Jobs has been involved with, the real genius of the man emerges. Georgia O'Keeffe said: "If an artist can come up with just *one* new idea…it's significant." Jobs has a whole basketful of innovations: Apple II, Lisa, Mac, NeXT, Pixar, iMac…with no end in sight. Along with the hardware and software that Jobs helped create are those astonishingly great advertising campaigns…but more on the advertising later. If you work anywhere in the graphic arts—advertising, design, photography, product design, even architecture—the person who has changed your life most profoundly was not an ad man, a designer, a photographer or an architect. It was Steve Jobs.

So we all breathed a huge sigh of relief when Jobs came riding back to Cupertino, and blew away the corporate dross that was strangling Apple. Most of us were having nightmares about the certainty of the gradual dilution of graphics quality in our daily lives. We could visualize "Chairman Bill" Gates sitting in Fortress MSFT, asking irritably "Just how many art directors *are* there, anyway?" If Gates ran the artistic/graphics world, we could all kiss quality goodbye. We know, even if America's corporate world *still* doesn't get it, that there are two kinds of computer users: those who use Macs and those who don't. And we know we owe a lot of our success to Steve Jobs.

Do we think Steve Jobs personally invented every pixelated image, every motherboard or software program that went into Apple? Hardly. Stephen Wozniak was the hacker/genius who gets credit for the first Apple (which, remember, *followed* the Altair). When Jobs joined his old buddy at Wozniak's "Homebrew Computer Club" to talk computers and where they might go, it was The Woz who came up with an effective floppy disk that instantly separated Apple from its competitors. A young software writer said: "His designs were like poems." But Jobs properly gets the credit for being the quarterback and the out-front guy. And for thinking up the Lisa (Lisa? read on), and then driving the Mac to it's enormous, breakthrough success. The Mac became The Computer For The Rest Of Us.

Jobs is not an "engineer" in the stereotypical, cold-blooded, hyper-analytical, devoid of graphic vision sense. Jobs is unique because of his crystal-clear vision of potential outcomes, blended with a rarely found, innate aesthetic sensibility, that's coupled with an iron determination to ship nothing less than quality products. "Real designers ship!" And Jobs has the guts to take risks. Big risks.

If Steve Jobs had never been born, it is undeniable that graphically, our world would be greatly diminished from where it is today. The internet would still be for academics; the World Wide Web might not even exist. And most ironically, there would certainly not be a Windows! At least not in the form we see it today—which, at best is still a shoddy Mac rip-off.

Jobs is thought of as "difficult." And "different." Certainly his temperament has been…*mercurial*. Are we surprised? Guys like Steve Jobs do not suffer fools lightly; Jobs likes and surrounds himself with people who know what they're talking about. A famous quote: "Jobs thinks people are either Brilliant or Bozos." In his biography of Jobs, Jeffrey Young says "Jobs has always had an amazing ability to put his ideas and overall vision into words—quotable, inspiring words. He could say what engineers and programmers only dream about." And he couples this vision with a kick-ass desire to do the job right…over and over again, until it is perfect. It pisses people off. It wears others out.

"Steve is like a good poker player. He'll go around to five or six people with the same idea, as if he had already made up his mind, but he's watching their eyes to see how they react." And he's always had an eye for great products, like the "Bauhaus" Braun products, Mercedes-Benz cars, the Cuisinart…you get the picture. His intense knowledge of topics *outside* computers, such as art and architecture, is truly unusual among industry leaders.

In a great leader, mental toughness is a vital ingredient, and Steve Jobs is really tough when it counts. At Pixar, they still talk with awe at how he faced down Michael Eisner, the Piranha-like Boss of The Mouse Factory. Millions of dollars were at

We rewrote the book.

The Powerbook G3 takes the world by storm.

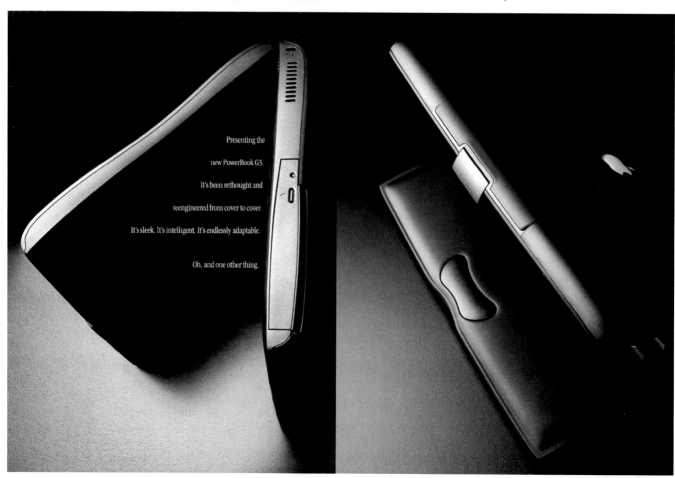

Presenting the
new PowerBook G3.
It's been rethought and
reengineered from cover to cover.
It's sleek. It's intelligent. It's endlessly adaptable.

Oh, and one other thing.

It eats Pentium notebooks for lunch.

The PowerPC™ G3 chip is a certifiable speed demon. In the latest BYTEmark integer tests (see convincing scores below), it's up to three times faster than the Pentium chips used in PC notebooks. In fact, even the most affordable PowerBook G3 beats the pants off the fastest Compaq notebook.

BYTEmark Integer Index Scores

PowerBook G3/292	9.8
PowerBook G3/250	8.4
PowerBook G3/233	7.3
Compaq Armada Pentium/266 MMX	2.9

See how your favorite colors (and a few million others) look on one of the brightest screens in a notebook—in full 1024-by-768 glory.

You'll need a better excuse than "my battery ran out." Add an optional second lithium-ion battery and you'll get up to seven hours of power under normal use. And just so you know where you stand juice-wise, there's a nifty LED indicator on each battery pack.

$2,299. That's the startling starting price for a new PowerBook G3, with two expansion bays and 20x CD-ROM drive. And yes, the battery is included.

Versatility, thy name is PowerBook. Every model comes with two built-in expansion bays (which also double as battery bays), as well as two very handy PC Card slots.

Exploit the media. You can "hot swap" at whim—with your choice of floppy and CD-ROM drives, or the optional DVD-ROM and third-party Zip drives.

Our keyboard engineers (yes, we have keyboard engineers) insisted on precision scissor-action keys. It's a long story, but trust us—they feel great.

The PowerBook G3 offers a full array of networking and communications ports, as well as 24-bit video-out. However you choose to link up to the world, via Ethernet or optional K56flex modem, it's a case of ready, aim, plug. No adapters needed.

*Estimated retail price. †On 13.3" and 14.1" models.

stake and Jobs would not be intimidated by Disney's power, which is part of the reason he became the youngest person ever to make the *Forbes* magazine list of richest people. And Jobs has more decorations for quality engineering than a Soviet Field Marshall. Today, between Apple and Pixar, Steve Jobs is actually running *two* major companies. Part of the time he's at Apple, part of the time at Pixar. Pixar has opened up new vistas for animators, based on massive, leading-edge technology. What took a factory-full of animators working by hand for months in the old days of *Fantasia* can now be done incredibly quickly using Pixar's whirring computers. They use *terabytes* of power, light years ahead of the industry.

Then there is Jobs, the quintessential Showman. Nobody can warm up a crowd of Mac lovers like Steve Jobs. Or better explain the latest innovative break-throughs. That's because he truly cares about the smallest details. Mies van der Rohe said that "God is in the details." Jobs is the rare businessman who takes that sort of ideal to heart.

In an interview with *Time* magazine, Jobs casually cited Leonardo da Vinci and Michelangelo as inspirations, reflecting his artistic side. Then he quoted Dr. Edwin Land's famous statement: "I want Polaroid to stand at the intersection of art and science," and says of Sony's Akio Morita: "He expressed his love for the human species in every product he made." Apple's scientific staff operated more like artists than engineers. No Clydesdale-type engineers from Hewlett-Packard at the Appleworks. Jobs has said that he sees himself as something like the Henry Ford of the computer industry. Ford's great insight was paying his workers enough to be able to afford the cars they made. Jobs simply wanted to make his computers the VWs of the computer industry. In other words, one person, one computer. Again...no wonder the graphic world idolizes the man.

Steve Jobs has never wavered from absolute design excellence. As he said in a famous 1991 *Fortune* interview: "Tens of millions of PC owners needlessly work with computers that are far less than they should be." Apple's head designer Jonathan Ive says: "The first time I used a Mac, it was so clear that somebody had paid attention to details that nobody else would have noticed. I remember thinking, 'That's remarkable. Why did they care so much?'"

Just before Jobs returned to Apple, Ive was in a dead-end job there with no prospects of a breakout, and was about to quit. Jobs came back and in mere months the iMac emerged. What changed the Apple that Ive knew? Steve Jobs. The paycheck still read Apple, but the inspiration was all Jobs. This genius has been apparent from the beginning.

When Jobs took his team into Xerox PARC in early 1980,

the Xerox people had no idea what to do with what they had developed. Jobs instantly saw the consumer-friendly possibilities of the mouse, using "point and click" as a means to get where you needed to go instead of having to type in tortured strings of impossible to remember commands. And he's never wavered from that core insight. Today's iMac was conceived as the quintessential "plug and play" computer that lets you browse the Internet in 10 minutes!

The Apple story started back in the 1970s, when Jobs and The Woz were tinkering with their embryonic computer in Jobs' parent's garage. Changes were in the air—big, profound changes, that centered on challenging authority wherever it was found. People were asking questions. Seeking their own answers. Sum it up as a desire to empower the individual.

Enter Steve Jobs and the personal computer. Personal computers could be the key to the dreamed of cultural revolution. Once an individual could employ the power of a personal computer, he or she would no longer be dependent upon centralized authority (read massive main-frame computers, locked away in air-conditioned fortresses, inaccessible to all but the specially anointed). In the 1970's, nothing epitomized centralized, authoritarian mentality better than IBM.

Steve Jobs was the perfect leader for the Computer Revolution. He'd dropped out of Reed College and gone tripping through India. We can imagine him soaking up that wildly colorful and creative environment. Perhaps that experience planted a seed that, years later, would emerge in the candy colored iMacs. As Picasso said: "Every idea has a father and a mother." Even then, the new computer company's name, Apple, has an anti-establishment flavor. Imagine naming a new *computer* after a common fruit?

An eclectic mind like Job's would be thinking metaphorically. The beginning of knowledge? Bingo: The Garden of Eden. The first bite (byte, actually)...(forbidden knowledge!) and we have a logo—a logo about as far removed from the ultra-corporate IBM logo as can be imagined.

The Apple II was the first real step toward consumer-friendly personal computing. And as far as it went, it was fine. But the Lisa was the breakthrough. Although the Lisa was not a commercial success, it introduced many of the key elements that were to spell eventual success for the Mac. Creating a workable Lisa wasn't easy. There was often no roadmap, since the Lisa team was flying blind in the realm of pure, ground-breaking creativity. The Lisa was the first to use a menu bar, the one-button mouse, the Clipboard, the Trash can. The first to let you point and drag, open by double-clicking, and let you watch windows zoom into overlapping views. Even figuring out simple, understandable

The beginning of knowledge? Bingo: The Garden of Eden. The first bite (byte, actually)... (forbidden knowledge!) and we have a logo....

"When we showed the [1984] spot to Apple's Board... there was a stunned silence. Then one of them asked: 'Are we looking for a new ad agency?'"

language to identify these features was surprisingly difficult.

To signal the revolution going on inside, Jobs had a black skull and crossbones hoisted over the Mac buildings. Then he spent a cool $100 million on development costs. They built a glistening new automated factory to produce the Macs, modelled after a superbly designed Canon plant in Japan. Remember, this was the 1980s, when Japan was kicking America's butt. Jobs toured over 100 factories in Japan to see for himself how they were doing it better.

When the Mac emerged, it changed the world of graphics forever. Before the Mac, we could go to a printer or output house and experiment with revising and altering images on-screen. In those days, however, the actual work was done by trained technicians using huge and very expensive equipment. And woe betide you if you didn't have an ample budget for costly over-runs! Changing the color of an eyeball could be done quickly or it could turn out to be a black hole; it all depended on the operator. Now, with the Mac, we can open Quark and Photoshop and change eyeballs, switch heads, add flying toasters or do virtually anything else we can imagine. All by ourselves! Most of us never took a single Mac class. One 15 year old says: "I taught myself Photoshop by sitting down at my computer and hitting every button. I watched what happened and it didn't take very long to figure out what to do."

Consider the formidable competition when the Mac was launched. The so-called Installed Base of IBM computers meant that IBM had a virtual lock on the most lucrative part of the market—the business segment. That left education, average consumers, and, of course, the graphics niche. Part of Jobs' method in bringing Apple back to life on his second tour of duty, is the seductive appeal of the colorful iMac line. At this year's Consumer Electronics Show, suddenly every other manufacturer seemed to be showing candy-colored products that ape iMac's color palette. Where before there had been some timid mini-steps toward broadening the color range, suddenly there are multitudes of multi-colored digital cameras, VCRs, TV sets, mice and keyboards. It took gutsy Steve Jobs to "give permission" to the world to lighten up, brighten up and bring some color into the office. (One definition of genius: being able to anticipate the future).

When Steve Jobs went looking for an advertising agency, he tapped Chiat/Day. Jay Chiat had the savvy street smarts and the tough moxie to stay at the table with Jobs. And Jay could deliver the creative horsepower needed to produce great advertising. Here's an insight for you: Steve Jobs worked *directly* with Jay Chiat and Chiat/Day on the campaigns. No ad manager intervened. Of the ad strategy, Jobs said, "We really agonize over

communications because we always want to do the right thing, and we want to do it well. We see design as a four-fold effort: one, graphics; two, advertising; three, what appears on the screen; and four, the design of the product itself. We feel we're breaking ground in all four of them." (P.S.: They still are.)

The result of this close collaboration was the famed "1984" TV spot. Steve loved it. But as Jay Chiat recites: "When we showed the spot to Apple's Board of Directors shortly before the Superbowl, there was a stunned silence. Then one of them asked: "Are we looking for a new ad agency?" This spot aired just *once*…during the 1984 Super Bowl. The next day, $6.5 million worth of Macs were sold in just 4 hours. Chiat/Day kept the account.

Despite the almost insurmountable difficulties it faced, Apple was still determined to break into the corporate world. They had literally been frozen out by IBM's absolute strangle-hold on the main-frame mentality of Fortune 500 *execunerds*. Steve Hayden says: "Then we produced the Lemmings commercial" (the successor to "1984", and a very tough act to follow). "We heard about noisy bars turning dead quiet when the spot was aired…and then boisterous cheering when it finished."

Eventually, Apple's growing international sales forced a review…which Chiat/Day blew. The agency team was sullen and demoralized; they couldn't believe Apple would walk away from them after their great years together. But when Jobs returned to Apple for Round Two, he immediately brought back Lee Clow and Chiat/Day. They, in turn, promptly delivered the now famous "Think Different" campaign. Was this because of Lee? Or Jobs? Or was it really Lee *plus* Jobs, working together again with their cutting-edge thinking on the current Apple problem? "Think Different" is pure advertising. Not a comma is wasted. Forget glossy four-color ads. They get blown away by the hypnotic affect of all those rebellious (and great) thinkers, who are perfect visual metaphors for the original, and continuing, Macintosh Vision.

The entire advertising business should take note. Despite all the ads, campaigns, hype and hot air…it IS still possible to do great advertising. Which is what Jay Chiat set out to do. And what Lee Clow (uniquely) is *still* able to do. On demand. What more is there to say? Inspirational client. Terrific agency responding with the kind of advertising most agencies can only fantasize about. "It's almost scary the way Steve can criticize an ad and be very much on the money. I'm sure he's the highest paid art director in America," said Apple creative director Tom Hughes.

Thank you Lee. And, especially, thank you Steve Jobs. Using Steve Jobs's favorite accolade: "Insanely great."

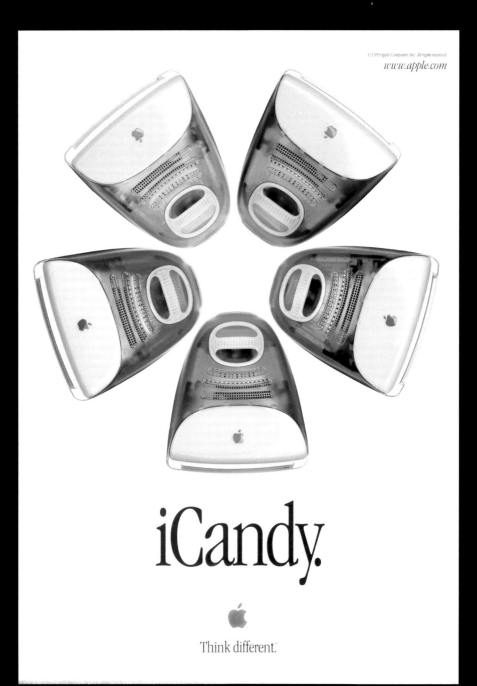

www.apple.com

iCandy.

Think different.

USweb/CKS's ad featuring the "…seductive appeal of the colorful iMac line."

Was wäre, wenn es einen Steve Jobs nie gegeben hätte?
von DickCalderhead

Mies van der Rohe sagte einmal, Gott sitze im Detail. Jobs ist einer der wenigen Unternehmer, die sich ein solches Ideal zu Herzen nehmen.

Millionen von Dollars standen auf dem Spiel, aber Jobs liess sich von Disneys Macht nicht beeindruken.

«Der Fall einer amerikanischen Ikone.»
Business Week, August, 1997

«Einen zweiten Akt gibt es in einem amerikanischen Leben nicht.»
Francis Scott Fitzgerald

«Es war ein Fehler von Apples Verwaltungsrat, es zuzulassen, dass der Geist vergangener Weihnachten, Steve Jobs, zurückkehrt. Es war nicht besonders klug, diesen Typen, der sich überall einmischt, auf Apple in der kritischsten Phase in der Firmengeschichte loszulassen.»
Jim Seymour, Kritiker, PC Magazine
Januar 1998

«Für Apple lässt sich durchaus noch etwas tun. Aber man müsste schon Gott engagieren, um das zu bewerkstelligen.»
Charles Haggerty, Handlungsbevollmächtigter, Western Digital
August, 1997

«Bezeichnenderweise muss ich bei einem Mac nie ein Handbuch knacken.»
Peter Lews, The New York Times

«Es hat mich schockiert, wie schnell das Publikum Windows geschluckt hat.....es ist ein fürchterliches, umständliches System.»
Nicholas Negroponte

«Steven Jobs zurückzuholen, war ein Riesenfehler. Sie wären gut beraten, die Stücke von Apple zu verkaufen... zum besten Preis, den sie kriegen können.»
Al «Kettensäge» Dunlop, Gefeuerter Handlungsbevollmächtigter,
Sunbeam, August, 1997

1997 waren sie bereit, Apple zu Grabe zu tragen. «Sie» waren die Firmenmanager, die Marketing-Leute und vor allem die Medien, speziell *Business Week* mit seiner Titelgeschichte. Doch die Unkenrufe waren verfrüht! Aus dem Scherbenhaufen, dem Desaster, in dem sich die Firma ohne Steve Jobs befand, hat sich Apple einmal mehr als dynamische, innovative Firma erhoben. Und mit dem iMac hat Apple einmal mehr den beliebtesten Computer für den Privatgebrauch in Amerika geschaffen. Während Investoren und «Firmenstrategen» drauf und dran waren, Apple zu zerstückeln und die Aktivposten um jeden Preis zu verkaufen, sah Steve Jobs die Dinge anders. Er wusste, was Apple retten würde, nämlich genau das, was den anfänglichen Erfolg ausgemacht hatte: Innovation. Jobs hatte einen ganzen Korb voller neuer Ideen: Apple II, Lisa, Mac, NeXt, Pixar, iMac., und ein Ende ist nicht in Sicht.

Die Hardware und Software, an deren Entwicklung Jobs beteiligt war, wurde zudem mit erstaunlich guten Werbekampgnen lanciert, aber mehr davon später. Wenn Sie mit Design zu tun haben – sei es in der Werbung, Graphik, Photographie, im Produktdesign oder in der Architektur – bei der Person, die Ihr Leben tiefgreifend verändert hat, handelt es sich weder um einen Werber, einen Designer, einen Photogaphen noch um einen Architekten: Es war Steve Jobs. Deshalb atmeten wir alle erleichtert auf, als Jobs nach Cupertino zurückkam und die betrieblichen Verstrickungen, die Apple zu ersticken drohten, beseitigte. Die meisten von uns hatten schon Alpträume hinsichtlich der zu erwartenden Verwässerung graphischer Qualität im täglichen Leben. Wir sahen bereits den Vorsitzenden Bill Gates in seiner MSFT-Festung vor uns, gereizt fragend: «Wie viele Art Direktoren gibt es denn überhaupt?» Wenn Gates in der Welt der Kunst und Graphik das Sagen hätte, könnten wir allesamt der Qualität Lebewohl sagen.

Auch wenn Amerikas Geschäftswelt es noch immer nicht begreifen will, es gibt zwei Arten von Computer-Anwendern – jene, die Macs benutzen, und jene, die das nicht tun. Und wir sind uns bewusst, dass wir einen grossen Teil unseres Erfolgs Steve Jobs verdanken. Stephen Wozniak war das Hackergenie, dem der erste Apple zu verdanken ist. (Erinnern Sie sich, der Apple folgte auf den Altair.) Als Steve sich mit seinem alten Freund Wozniak in dessen «Homebrew Computer Club» zusammentat und über Computer und ihre Zukunft sprach, war es Woz, der eine funktionierende Floppy Disk entwickelte, die Apple mit einem Schlag von der Konkurrenz unterschied. Ein junger Autor im Bereich Software sagte: «Seine Designs waren wie Gedichte.» Jobs hingegen übernahm den Part des Angreifers, des Mannes in der Öffentlichkeit. Und er hat sich Lisa ausgedacht (Lisa? Siehe unten) und dem Mac dann zu seinem enormen Durchbruch verholfen. Der Mac wurde der Computer für den Rest der Menschheit.

Jobs war kein Techniker im üblichen Sinne, kein kaltblütiger, analytischer Denker ohne eine graphische Vision. Jobs ist einzigartig wegen seiner kristallklaren Vision potentieller Ergebnisse, verbunden mit einem ungewöhnlichen, natürlichen Gefühl für Ästhetik und der eisernen Entschlossenheit, nur Qualitätsprodukte auf den Markt zu bringen. Und Jobs hat den Mut, Risiken einzugehen. Grosse Risiken.

Wenn es nie einen Steve Jobs gegeben hätte, wäre unsere Welt aus graphischer Sicht zweifellos ganz woanders, als wo sie heute ist. Das Internet wäre Akademikern vorbehalten; das World Wide Web gäbe es wahrscheinlich gar nicht. Und ironischerweise gäbe es ganz sicher kein Windows! Zumindest nicht in der Form, wie wir es heute kennen, denn es ist im Grunde eine schäbige Mac-Imitation.

Jobs gilt als schwierig. Und als anders. Sicherlich hat er eine sprunghafte Natur. Überrascht das? Typen wie Steve Jobs ertragen Idioten nur schwer; Jobs umgibt sich mit Leuten, die wissen, wovon sie reden. Ein berühmtes Zitat: «Jobs hält die Leute entweder für brillant oder für Idioten.»

In seiner Jobs-Biographie sagt Jeffrey Young: «Jobs hat die unglaubliche Gabe, seine Ideen und allgemeinen Visionen mitreissend und druckreif zu formulieren. Er kann sich auf eine

Weise ausdrücken, von der Techniker und Programmierer nur träumen können.» Und er verbindet seine Vision mit dem unbändigen Verlangen, etwas gut zu machen... unablässig an etwas zu arbeiten, bis es perfekt ist. Das macht die Leute verrückt, sie halten es nicht aus.

Für jemanden in führender Position ist geistige Stärke eine wichtige Voraussetzung, und Steve Jobs ist stark, wenn es darauf ankommt. Bei Pixar sprechen sie noch immer mit Hochachtung davon, wie er Michael Eisner, dem Boss von The Mouse Factory, der sich wie ein Piranha auf alles stürzt, die Stirn bot. Millionen von Dollars standen auf dem Spiel, aber Jobs liess sich von Disneys Macht nicht beeindrucken.

Heute leitet Steve Jobs mit Apple und Pixar praktisch zwei grosse Firmen. Er teilt seine Zeit einfach zwischen Apple und Pixar auf. Pixar hat der Animationsbranche auf der Basis weitreichender, hochmoderner Technologie neue Möglichkeiten eröffnet. Was in den Zeiten von *Fantasia* für eine ganze Halle von Animationszeichnern monatelange Handarbeit bedeutete, kann jetzt in unglaublich kurzer Zeit mit Pixars Computern bewerkstelligt werden. Sie sind in ihrer Kapazität der Konkurrenz um Lichtjahre voraus.

Jobs ist der Inbegriff eines Showmans. Niemand kann die Masse von Mac-Anhängern so begeistern oder die jüngsten bahnbrechenden Neuerungen so gut erklären wie Steve Jobs. Für ihn zählt auch das winzigste Detail. Mies van der Rohe sagte einmal, Gott sitze im Detail. Jobs ist einer der wenigen Unternehmer, die sich ein solches Ideal zu Herzen nehmen.

In einem Interview mit dem Magazin *Time* nannte der kunstbegeisterte Jobs ganz unbefangen Leonardo da Vinci und Michelangelo als Vorbilder. Dann zitierte er Dr. Edwin Lands berühmten Ausspruch: «Ich will, dass Polaroid an der Schnittstelle zwischen Kunst und Wissenschaft steht.» Über Akio Morita von Sony sagt er: «Jedes Produkt, das er machte, war Ausdruck seiner Liebe zu den Menschen.» Apples wissenschaftliche Mitarbeiter arbeiten eher wie Künstler als wie Techniker. Bei Apple findet man keine Techniker der robusten, sturen Sorte wie bei Hewlett-Packard.

Jobs hat einmal gesagt, er betrachte sich als den Henry Ford der Computerbranche. Ford war so klug, seinen Arbeitern genug zu bezahlen, dass sie sich die Autos, die sie herstellten, leisten konnten. Jobs wollte, dass seine Computer die «Volkswagen» der Branche werden. In anderen Worten, eine Person, ein Computer. Kein Wunder also, dass dieser Mann zum Idol der Graphikbranche wurde.

Steve Jobs hat sein Ideal vom absolut hervorragenden Design nie verraten. In dem inzwischen berühmten Interview in der Zeitschrift *Fortune* im Jahre 1991 sagte er: «Zehn Millionen von PC-Besitzern arbeiten ohne Grund mit Computern, die in keiner Weise dem entsprechen, was sie eigentlich sein sollten.» Apples Design-Chef Jonathan Ive sagt: «Als ich das erste Mal einen Mac benutzte, war mir klar, dass hier jemand auf Details geachtet hatte, die jedem anderen entgangen wären. Ich erinnere mich, dass ich dachte: «Das ist bemerkenswert. Warum haben sie sich solche Mühe gegeben?»»

Kurz bevor Jobs zu Apple zurückkehrte, befand sich Ive beruflich in einer Sackgasse, aus der es keinen Ausweg zu geben schien, und er hatte vor, Apple zu verlassen. Jobs kam zurück, und in nur wenigen Monaten war der iMac da. Was veränderte die Firma Apple, die Ive kennengelernt hatte? Steve Jobs! Die Firma, die Ive bezahlte, hiess noch immer Apple, aber die Inspiration kam von Jobs. Jobs hat sich von Anfang an als Genie erwiesen.

Als Jobs Anfang 1980 sein Team zu Xerox PARC brachte, hatten die Xerox-Leute keine Ahnung, was sie mit den Sachen, die sie entwickelt hatten, anfangen sollten. Jobs erkannte sofort, welche Erleichterungen die Maus dem Anwender bieten konnte, der jetzt nur noch markieren und klicken musste, um zu bekommen, was er wollte, statt die unendlichen Befehle, die sich niemand merken kann, mühsam einzugeben. Nie hat er sich in dieser Überzeugung beirren lassen. Der heutige iMac war im Grunde als ein Computer konzipiert, den man einfach an den Strom anschliessen muss, um damit spielen zu können und in zehn Minuten im Internet zu sein!

Die Apple-Geschichte begann in den Siebzigerjahren, als Jobs und «The Woz» alles Mögliche mit ihrem rudimentären Computer in der Garage von Jobs' Eltern ausprobierten. Veränderungen lagen in der Luft – grosse, tiefgreifende Veränderungen antiautoritärer Art. Die Menschen stellten Fragen und suchten ihre eigenen Antworten. Im Grunde ging es darum, die Position des Individuums zu stärken.

Dann trat Steve Jobs in Erscheinung und mit ihm der Personal Computer. Personal Computer konnten der Schlüssel der erträumten Kulturrevolution sein. Wenn ein Einzelner erst einmal mit dem Personal Computer umgehen konnte, hing er nicht mehr von der zentralen Autorität ab (sprich von den in klimatisierten Festungen unter Verschluss gehaltenen Riesenrechnern, die nur Auserwählten zugänglich waren). In den Siebzigerjahren verkörperte nichts und niemand diese zentralisierte, autoritäre Mentalität besser als IBM.

Steve Jobs war der perfekte Anführer der Computer-Revolution. Er hatte das College vorzeitig verlassen und sich nach Indien aufgemacht. Man kann sich vorstellen, wie er diese wilde, farbige, zutiefst kreative Umgebung förmlich aufsog. Vielleicht wurde hier der Samen für das gelegt, was Jahre später als bonbonfarbener Mac herauskommen sollte. Schon Picasso sagte: «Jede Idee hat einen Vater und eine Mutter.» Selbst der Name der neuen Computerfirma, Apple, hatte etwas Antiautoritäres. Man stelle sich vor, ein Computer, der nach einer ganz gewöhnlichen Frucht benannt wird!

Ein eklektischer Kopf wie der von Jobs dachte metaphorisch. Der Anfang allen Wissens? Das Paradies! Der erste Biss (bite oder genau genommen byte)...(verbotene Erkenntnis!), und wir haben ein Logo, das nicht weiter entfernt sein könnte von dem ultrakonservativen IBM-Logo.

Der Apple II war der erste wirkliche Schritt in Richtung eines anwenderfreundlichen Computers. Und er war gut. Aber Lisa war der Durchbruch. Obwohl Lisa kein kommerzieller Erfolg war, enthielt er viele der Schlüsselelemente, die später den Erfolg des Mac ausmachten. Es war nicht einfach, ein funktionierendes Modell von Lisa zu kreieren. Oft genug tappte man im Dunkeln, das Lisa-Team befand sich auf einem Blindflug im Bereich purer, bahnbrechender Kreativität. Bei Lisa gab es zum ersten Mal Symbolleisten, die Maus mit nur einem Knopf, das Clipboard, den Papierkorb. Zum ersten Mal konnte man etwas anklicken und verschieben, etwas durch einen Doppelklick öffnen und übereinander gelagerte Fenster einzeln hervorholen und anschauen. Überraschend schwer war es, eine einfache, verständliche Sprache zu finden, mit der man die neuen Eigenschaften bezeichnen konnte.

Um sichtbar zu machen, dass sich in den Mac-Gebäuden eine Revolution abspielte, liess Jobs draussen schwarze Piratenflaggen hissen. Er gab kaltblütig ganze 100 Millionen Dollar für Entwicklung aus. Sie bauten eine nagelneue automatisierte Fabrik für die Herstellung der Macs, nach dem Vorbild der hervorragend konzipierten Canon-Fabrik in Japan. Man erinnere sich: Das war in den Achtzigerjahren, als Japan Amerikas Wirtschaft das Fürchten lehrte. Jobs besuchte über 100 Fabriken in Japan, um selbst zu sehen, was sie besser machten.

Der Mac bedeutete eine tiefgreifende und unwiderrufliche Veränderung im Bereich der Gebrauchsgraphik. Bevor es ihn gab, konnte man zum Drucker oder zu einer Computerfirma gehen, wenn man am Bildschirm mit Bildern experimentieren oder sie überarbeiten bzw. verändern wollte. Zu jener Zeit jedoch wurde die tatsächliche Arbeit von ausgebildeten Technikern an riesigen, ungeheuer teuren Geräten gemacht. Und man war schlecht dran, wenn man nicht über ein grosses Budget für kostspielige Bearbeitungen verfügte. Wenn man die Farbe eines Augenpaars verändern wollte, konnte das relativ schnell gehen, es konnte sich aber ebensogut als Fass ohne Boden erweisen – das hing ganz von dem Techniker ab. Mit dem Mac können wir jetzt ganz einfach im Quark oder Photoshop Augenfarben verändern, Köpfe austauschen, fliegende Toaster hinzufügen - der Phantasie sind keine Grenzen gesetzt. Und wir können das selbst machen!

Man erinnere sich einmal daran, was die formidable Konkurrenz in der Zeit machte, als der Mac lanciert wurde. Die sogenannte «Installed Base» der IBM Computer bedeutete nichts anderes, als dass IBM den lukrativsten Teil des Marktes, den Geschäftssektor, fest unter Kontrolle hatte. Schulen, der Durchschnittsverbraucher und natürlich die Graphik-Branche waren völlig davon ausgeschlossen.

Als Jobs zum zweiten Mal bei Apple einstieg und die Firma wieder auf die Beine brachte, gehörte u.a. das verführerische Äussere der farbenfrohen iMac-Serie zu seiner Erfolgsmethode. Bei der diesjährigen Messe für Verbraucherelektronik warteten fast alle Hersteller mit bonbonfarbenen Produkten auf, ein Abklatsch der Farbpalette des iMacs. Wo man sich zuvor nur schüchtern in Richtung einer grösseren Farbpalette vorgewagt hatte, gab es jetzt Unmengen von sehr farbigen digitalen Kameras, Videorecordern, TV-Geräten, Mäusen und Tastaturen zu bestaunen. Es musste erst ein mutiger Steve Jobs auftauchen und der Welt bzw. den Büros die Erlaubnis geben, freundlicher und farbiger auszusehen.

Als sich Steve Jobs nach einer Werbeagentur umsah, entschied er sich für Chiat/Day. Jay Chiat war erfahren, ein guter Beobachter und Zuhörer, und er hatte das erforderliche Durchhaltevermögen, um Jobs gewachsen zu sein. Zudem verfügte Jay über die für grossartige Werbung erforderlichen kreativen Ressourcen.

Hiermit sei ausserdem verraten, dass Steve Jobs direkt mit Jay Chiat und der Agentur an den Kampagnen arbeitete. Kein Kundenbetreuer, der sich dazwischenschaltete. Was die Werbestrategie angeht, sagte Jobs damals: «Wir haben uns bezüglich der Kommunikation die Köpfe zermartert. Wir wollen immer das Richtige tun, und wir wollen es gut machen. Für uns gehören vier Dinge zum Design: erstens die Graphik, zweitens die Werbung, drittens das, was auf dem Bildschirm erscheint, und viertens das Design des Produktes selbst. Wir glauben, dass wir in jedem dieser Bereiche bahnbrechend sind.» (P.S. ...Sie sind es immer noch!)

Das Ergebnis dieser engen Zusammenarbeit war der inzwischen berühmt gewordene «1984»-TV Spot. Steve war begeistert. Aber Jay Chiat erzählt: «Als wir den Spot Apples Verwaltungsrat kurz vor der Ausstrahlung von Super Bowl (einer sehr beliebten Unterhaltungssendung) vorführten, herrschte betretenes Schweigen. Dann fragte einer von ihnen: «Suchen wir eine neue Werbeagentur?» Der Spot lief nur einmal...während der 1984 Super-Bowl-Sendung. Am folgenden Tag wurden innerhalb von nur vier Stunden Macs im Wert von 6,5 Millionen Dollar verkauft.» Chiat/Day blieb Apples Agentur.

Trotz der fast unüberwindlichen Schwierigkeiten war Apple nach wie vor entschlossen, sich die Geschäftswelt zu erobern. IBM hatte die Führungskräfte der fünfhundert grössten Firmen eisern im Griff, so dass ein Eindringen in diesen Markt fast ausgeschlossen war. Steven Hayden sagt: «Dann produzierten wir den «Lemmings»-Spot (den Nachfolger von «1984», was keine leichte Aufgabe war). Uns wurde von lauten Bars berichtet, in denen Totenstille herrschte, sobald der Spot lief ...gefolgt von jubelndem Beifall.»

Als Apples Verkäufe auch ausserhalb Amerikas zunahmen, wurde eine Überarbeitung der Werbung notwendig – und Chiat/Day vermasselte sich die Chance. (Das Agenturteam war enttäuscht und demoralisiert; sie konnten einfach nicht glauben, dass Apple sie nach so vielen Jahren erfolgreicher Zusammenarbeit fallen lassen würde. Als Jobs jedoch zu Apple für Runde Zwei zurückkehrte, holte er sofort auch Lee Clow und Chiat/Day zurück. Diese wiederum lieferten prompt die heute berühmte «Think-Different»-Kampagne. War das Lee Clow zu verdanken? Oder Jobs? Oder vielmehr Lee Clow plus Jobs, die zusammen auf ihre Art über das aktuelle Problem von Apple nachdachten?

«Think Different» ist Werbung in Reinkultur. Kein überflüssiges Komma, nichts. Keine Rede von farbiger Hochglanzwerbung. Derartige Anzeigen haben keine Chance angesichts der hypnotischen Wirkung der rebellischen (und grossen) Denker, die in der Werbung gezeigt werden - ausgezeichnete visuelle Metaphern für die nach wie vor originelle Macintosh-Vision. Die Werbewelt sollte sich das vor Augen halten. Trotz der Flut von Anzeigen, Kampagnen, dem jugendlichen Getue und trotz viel heisser Luft: Es IST noch immer möglich, grossartige Werbung zu machen. Jay Chiat hat es bewiesen, und Lee Clow ist noch immer dazu in der Lage, und zwar auf Bestellung.

Was wäre noch hinzuzufügen? Ein inspirierender Kunde. Eine ausgezeichnete Agentur, die auf diesen Kunden mit einer Werbung reagiert, von der andere nur träumen. «Die Art, wie Steve eine Anzeige kritisieren und das Geld zusammenhalten kann, ist fast beängstigend. Ich bin sicher, er ist der höchstbezahlte Art Director in Amerika,» sagt Tom Hughes, Creative Director bei Apple.

Danke, Lee Clow. Und ganz besonders, danke, Steve Jobs. Um es mit Steve Jobs' Lieblingsworten zu sagen: «Wahnsinnig gut!»

Et comment serait le monde si Steve Jobs n'existait pas?
par Dick Calderhead

«La chute d'une icône américaine»
Business Week, Août 1997

«Il n'y a pas de deuxième acte dans la vie des Américains.»
Francis Scott Fitzgerald

«Le conseil d'administration d'Apple a commis une erreur en permettant à Steve Jobs, fantôme resurgi lors des dernières fêtes de Noël, de revenir sur le devant de la scène. Donner carte blanche à ce touche-à-tout au moment le plus crucial de l'histoire d'Apple, voilà une décision qui manque sérieusement de bon sens.»
Jim Seymour, Critique au PC Magazine
Janvier 1998

«Apple a toujours de belles opportunités. Mais c'est Dieu qu'il faudrait engager pour faire le travail.»
Charles Haggerty, CEO, Western Digital
Août 1997

«Ce qui est typique avec un Mac, c'est que je ne dois jamais metre mon nez dans un manuel.»
Peter Lews, The New York Times

«J'ai été choqué de constater avec quelle rapidité le public a gobé Windows ... un horrible système et compliqué en plus.»
Nicholas Negroponte

«Rappeler Steve Jobs a été une erreur monumentale. Mon conseil... vendez Apple en pièces détachées ... au meilleur prix possible!»
Al Dunlop, Ancien CEO de Sunbeam, renvoyé par son employeur
Août 1997

En 1997, ils étaient prêts à enterrer Apple. Ils étant les directeurs de la société, les pros du marketing et notamment les médias avec, en tête de file, *Business Week* et sa couverture assassine. Mais pas si vite. Des cendres d'un désastre, là où se trouvait Apple sans Steve Jobs, le phénix a réussi à renaître, encore plus vibrant et lumineux. Et avec le iMac, Apple détient une fois de plus l'ordinateur préféré des Américains.

Tandis que les investisseurs et les stratèges de l'entreprise étaient tout disposés à morceler Apple et à en brader les actifs pour une bouchée de pain, faute de mieux, Steve Jobs voyait les choses sous un autre angle. Lui, il connaissait le secret pour sauver Apple et ce secret n'était rien d'autre que ce qui avait rendu la société si florissante à ses débuts: l'innovation. Pas étonnant, dès lors, que Steve Jobs soit tenu en si haute estime par les créatifs du monde entier.

Si vous pensez à toutes les grandes percées technologiques qui portent l'empreinte de Steve Jobs, alors vous saisissez le génie de cet homme. Georgia O'Keefe a déclaré: «Si un artiste trouve une seule idée nouvelle ... c'est considérable.» Steve Jobs, lui, a des idées nouvelles à revendre: Apple II, Lisa, Mac, NeXT, Pixar, iMac... Et son esprit inventif n'est pas près de s'épuiser.

Le matériel et les logiciels créés avec la collaboration de Steve Jobs ont en outre été lancés avec d'étonnantes campagnes publicitaires... Mais nous y reviendrons plus tard.

Si vous travaillez dans le domaine créatif, peu importe la discipline – publicité, graphisme, photographie, design de produits, voire architecture – la personne qui a le plus profondément changé votre vie n'est pas un publicitaire, un photographe ou un architecte. C'est Steve Jobs.

Aussi avons-nous tous poussé un ouf de soulagement en apprenant que Steve Jobs avait repris le chemin de Cupertino et éliminé tous les goulets d'étranglement qui menaçaient d'asphyxier définitivement Apple. La plupart d'entre nous faisaient des cauchemars, sachant que la qualité du graphisme baisserait graduellement dans nos vies quotidiennes. C'est que nous Bill Gates assis dans sa forteresse MSFT, demandant d'un air irrité: «Mais combien existe-t-il imaginions donc de directeurs artistiques?» Si Gates dirigeait le monde des arts graphiques, nous pourrions dire adieu à la qualité.

Même si les entrepreneurs américains ne l'ont toujours pas compris, nous, nous savons que les utilisateurs d'ordinateurs se divisent en deux catégories: ceux qui ne jurent que par le Mac et les autres. Et nous savons aussi que nous devons une large part de notre succès à Steve Jobs.

Mais Steve Jobs serait-il l'inventeur de chaque image composée de milliers de pixels, de chaque carte mère ou logiciel utilisés pour un produit Apple? Certainement pas. C'est en fait Stephen Wozniak, pirate et génie passionné d'informatique, qui est à l'origine du premier Apple lequel, rappelez-vous, succéda à l'Altair. Steve passait certes beaucoup de temps au Homebrew Computer Club (club d'ordinateurs faits maison) de son vieux pote The Woz pour parler d'informatique et de projets d'avenir, mais ce fut The Woz qui développa un disque souple – invention grâce à laquelle Apple se démarqua aussitôt de ses concurrents. Un jeune auteur spécialisé dans les logiciels a dit un jour: «Ses designs étaient comme des poèmes.» Steve Jobs, par contre, est connu pour être le fin stratège, l'homme aux avant-postes. Et aussi celui qui a eu l'idée de Lisa (Lisa? nous y reviendrons également plus tard) et a permis à Apple de percer sur le marché pour devenir une entreprise au succès phénoménal. Puis le reste de l'humanité a adopté le Mac.

Steve Jobs n'est pas un ingénieur au sens stéréotypé du terme, un concepteur à l'esprit analytique et froid dénué de toute notion graphique. Il est unique parce qu'il a une vision cristalline des potentiels à exploiter et un sens inné et rare de l'esthétique. Qui plus est, il est intraitable sur la qualité des produits et a le courage de prendre des risques. De gros risques.

Si Steve Jobs n'avait jamais vu le jour, il est indéniable que le monde graphique ne serait pas là où il est aujourd'hui. L'Internet serait réservé aux académiciens et peut-être même que la Toile n'existerait pas. Et, ironiquement, Windows serait sans doute inconnu! Ou du moins sous sa forme actuelle, car c'est en

A sample from TBWA Chiat-Day's influential "Think Different" capmaign.

Think different.

www.apple.com

Think different.

www.apple.com

Think different.

COURAGEOUS

www.apple.com

Think different.

www.apple.com

Mies van der Rohe a déclaré que «Dieu est dans le détail.» Steve Jobs est l'un des rares entrepreneurs qui prenne à cœur ce genre d'idéal.

«Jobs pense que les gens sont soit brillants ou stupides.»

fait une imitation bon marché du Mac.

Steve Jobs a la réputation d'être difficile et différent. Il est d'ailleurs connu pour ses sautes d'humeur. Mais est-ce surprenant? Des hommes de la trempe de Steve Jobs ne supportent pas les idiots; il s'entoure de personnes qui savent de quoi elles parlent. Pour mieux situer le personnage, une citation le concernant: «Jobs pense que les gens sont soit brillants ou stupides.»

Dans sa biographie consacrée à l'artisan d'Apple, Jeffrey Young a écrit: «Jobs a cette faculté incroyable de pouvoir formuler ses idées et visions en des termes qui interpellent et restent gravés dans les esprits. Son langage ne peut que faire rêver les ingénieurs et programmateurs.» Et ses visions sont associées à cette volonté farouche de produire de la qualité, de travailler sans relâche à un projet jusqu'à ce que le résultat soit parfait. Cette persévérance a le don d'agacer les gens, de mettre leurs nerfs à vif.

«Steve est comme un bon joueur de poker. Il présentera la même idée à cinq ou six personnes – comme s'il avait déjà pris sa décision – et les regardera dans les yeux pour observer leur réaction.» Et il a toujours eu un œil pour les bons produits, tels que les articles Bauhaus de Braun ou les Mercedes-Benz. En outre, ses vastes connaissances sur des sujets étrangers à l'informatique, comme l'art ou l'architecture, font de lui une figure d'exception dans sa branche.

Pour une personne qui occupe une fonction dirigeante, avoir un mental fort est essentiel. Et Steve Jobs sait faire montre de cette qualité lorsque la situation l'exige. Les collaborateurs de Pixar parlent encore, avec une admiration non dissimulée, de ce jour où il a tenu tête au grand boss de The Mouse Factory, une sorte de piranha qui dévore tout sur son passage. Des millions de dollars étaient en jeu, et Jobs ne se laissa pas le moins du monde intimider par la puissance de Disney. Cela explique en partie pourquoi Steve Jobs est la plus jeune personne à avoir figuré à ce jour sur la liste des grosses fortunes du magazine *Forbes*. Et il possède plus de décorations pour ses prouesses d'ingénieur que n'importe quel officier soviétique.

Aujourd'hui, avec Apple et Pixar, Steve Jobs dirige deux grandes compagnies. Il partage son temps entre les deux sociétés. Dans la branche de l'animation, Pixar a ouvert de nouveaux horizons grâce à des technologies de pointe aux possibilités quasi illimitées. S'il fallait autrefois, pour un film comme *Fantasia*, toute une armada de dessinateurs travaillant «d'arrache-main» durant des mois, aujourd'hui, les ordinateurs superperformants de Pixar permettent d'obtenir le même résultat en un rien de temps. En termes de capacité, ils ont des années-lumière d'avance sur la concurrence.

Steve Jobs est un showman par excellence. Personne ne parvient à enthousiasmer autant que lui les accros du Mac. Ou à mieux expliquer les dernières innovations apportées à un produit. C'est parce que pour lui, chaque détail compte. Mies van der Rohe a déclaré que «Dieu est dans le détail». Steve Jobs est l'un des rares entrepreneurs qui prenne à cœur ce genre d'idéal.

Dans une interview accordée au magazine *Time*, le passionné d'art Steve Jobs a cité le plus naturellement du monde Léonard de Vinci et Michel-Ange comme ses exemples. Puis il a prononcé une phrase célèbre d'Edwin Land: «Je veux que Polaroïd se trouve à l'intersection de l'art et de la science». D'Akio Morita de Sony, il dit: «Cet homme a exprimé son amour de l'humanité dans chacun de ses produits.» Les scientifiques au service d'Apple travaillent plutôt comme des artistes que des ingénieurs. Il n'y a pas de techniciens pur jus comme chez Hewlett-Packard par exemple.

Steve Jobs a dit un jour qu'il se voyait un peu comme le Henry Ford de l'industrie informatique. D'une intelligence rare, Ford payait suffisamment bien ses employés pour qu'ils puissent acheter les voitures sorties de l'usine. Steve Jobs a simplement voulu faire de ses ordinateurs les VW de l'industrie informatique. En d'autres termes, une personne, un ordinateur. Une autre raison qui explique pourquoi il est l'idole du monde graphique.

Steve Jobs n'a jamais trahi son idéal d'excellence en matière de design. Dans un entretien, entre-temps célèbre, paru dans le magazine Fortune en 1991, il a déclaré: «Dix millions de propriétaires de PC travaillent sans raison aucune avec des ordinateurs qui sont loin d'être ce qu'ils devraient être.» Le designer en chef d'Apple Jonathan Ive raconte: «La première fois que j'ai utilisé un Mac, j'ai tout de suite remarqué que quelqu'un avait accordé une attention particulière à des détails que personne d'autre n'aurait remarqués. Je me souviens avoir pensé, «C'est génial. Pourquoi se sont-ils donné tant de peine?»»

Juste avant que Steve Jobs ne retourne chez Apple, Ive se trouvait professionnellement dans un cul-de-sac, apparemment sans issue. Il avait l'intention de donner sa démission. Puis Steve Jobs est revenu et, en l'espace de quelques mois, le iMac est né. Qu'est-ce qui a changé la société Apple, telle qu'Ive la connaissait? Steve Jobs. L'entreprise qui payait son salaire s'appelait toujours Apple, mais l'inspiration venait de Steve Jobs. Dès le début, Steve Jobs s'est illustré par son génie.

Lorsqu'au début des années 1980, Steve Jobs s'est rendu avec son équipe chez Xerox PARC, les gens de Xerox n'avaient pas la moindre idée de ce qu'ils allaient bien pouvoir faire avec les dernières idées développées par leurs soins. Steve Jobs reconnut aussitôt les avantages de la souris, avec laquelle il suffisait maintenant de marquer et de cliquer pour effectuer une opération, au lieu d'entrer laborieusement quantité de commandes dont personne ne parvenait de toute façon à se souvenir. Et il n'a jamais démordu de cette idée maîtresse: la simplicité. Le iMac a été conçu comme un ordinateur que l'on doit brancher sur une prise de courant avant de commencer à jouer avec et de surfer sur Internet en l'espace de dix minutes!

La success story d'Apple a débuté dans les années 1970, lorsque Steve Jobs et The Woz passaient le plus clair de leur temps à faire des expériences avec leur ordinateur rudimentaire dans le garage des parents de Steve Jobs. A l'époque, les changements étaient à l'ordre du jour, des changements importants, fondamentaux, qui iraient à l'encontre de toute forme d'autorité. Les gens se posaient des questions et cherchaient à y apporter leurs propres réponses. En résumé: il s'agissait de renforcer la position de l'individu.

Arrivèrent Steve Jobs et l'ordinateur individuel. Les micro-ordinateurs seraient peut-être la clé de cette révolution culturelle tant espérée. Dès le moment où une personne parvenait à utiliser un micro-ordinateur, elle n'était plus dépendante de l'autorité centrale, à savoir ces énormes ordinateurs enfermés dans des forteresses climatisées uniquement accessibles à quelques privilégiés. Dans les années 1970, rien ni personne ne symbolisait mieux cette mentalité autoritaire et centralisée qu'IBM.

Steve Jobs présentait le profil idéal pour révolutionner le monde des ordinateurs. Il avait interrompu ses études supérieures avant de prendre le chemin de l'Inde. On peut imaginer à quel point il s'est imprégné de ces paysages sauvages aux couleurs chatoyantes. Peut-être est-ce à ce moment qu'une petite graine a été plantée, un germe qui a donné des années plus tard un gros bonbon aux délicieuses couleurs appelé iMac. Picasso ne disait-il pas que chaque idée a un père et une mère? Rien que le nom d'Apple avait déjà quelque chose d'antiautoritaire. Imaginez un ordinateur qui porte le nom d'un fruit des plus ordinaires. Un esprit aussi éclectique que celui de Job pensait par métaphores. La preuve:

D'où la connaissance tire-t-elle son origine? Du jardin d'Eden.Et à quel fait marquant fait penser ce paradis? A la morsure (bite en anglais, ou plus précisément byte) dans la pomme, autrement dit à la connaissance interdite. Et c'est ainsi qu'est né un logo – un logo qui ne pourrait être plus à l'opposé de celui, ultraconservateur, d'IBM.

L'Apple II fut le premier pas vers un micro-ordinateur convivial. Et il l'était vraiment. Mais la véritable révolution vint avec Lisa. Bien que Lisa ne fût pas un succès commercial, cet ordinateur présentait de nombreuses composantes qui allaient faire la réussite du Mac. Développer un modèle fonctionnel de Lisa ne fut pas une mince affaire. Souvent, l'équipe chargée du projet tâtonnait dans le noir dans la mesure où elle avançait à l'aveugle dans un monde de créativité pure, de créativité révolutionnaire. Lisa fut le premier ordinateur à utiliser une barre de menu, une souris à bouton unique, un clipboard et une poubelle. Et le premier aussi avec lequel on pouvait cliquer et déplacer, ouvrir en double-cliquant et aller chercher des fenêtres superposées et les regarder. Ce fut extrêmement difficile de créer un langage simple et compréhensible pour désigner ces nouvelles fonctions.

Pour signaler qu'une révolution se préparait dans les bâtiments Apple, Steve Jobs fit placer pavillons de corsaire à l'extérieur. Puis il investit, sans sourciller, 100 millions de dollars dans le développement. Pour la production des Mac, une fabrique automatisée flambant neuve fut construite sur le modèle d'une usine Canon implantée au Japon, dont le concept se distinguait par son ingéniosité. Souvenez-vous, c'était les années 1980, lorsque les Japonais faisaient trembler l'économie américaine. Steve Jobs visita 100 fabriques japonaises pour connaître les raisons de leur réussite.

L'arrivée du Mac sur le marché changea à jamais le domaine du graphisme utilitaire. Avant, on se rendait chez l'imprimeur ou une société informatique lorsqu'on désirait retravailler des images à l'écran ou faire des expériences. Le véritable travail était effectué par des techniciens chevronnés qui utilisaient des équipements aussi onéreux qu'imposants. Et pour procéder aux retouches ultérieures, il valait mieux disposer d'un budget important. Changer la couleur d'un globe oculaire pouvait ne

prendre qu'un instant ou se transformer en véritable cauchemar selon les compétences du technicien. Aujourd'hui, avec le Mac, il suffit d'ouvrir QuarkXPress ou Photoshop pour effectuer soi-même ces modifications, échanger des visages, ajouter des toasters volants… L'imagination ne connaît plus de limites! La plupart d'entre nous n'ont jamais suivi un cours Mac. Un adolescent de 15 ans a déclaré: «J'ai appris à me servir tout seul de Photoshop. Je me suis assis à mon ordinateur et j'ai essayé tous les boutons. Je regardais ce qui se passait et j'ai très vite appris ce qu'il fallait faire.»

Rappelons-nous aussi les manigances de la concurrence lorsque le Mac fut lancé. Ce que l'on appelait l'Installed Base des ordinateurs IBM signifiait tout simplement qu'IBM avait mis la main sur la partie la plus lucrative du marché – le segment des affaires. Il restait donc l'éducation, l'utilisateur moyen et, bien entendu, la niche du graphisme.

Lorsque Steve Jobs a fait son second tour de piste pour remettre Apple sur les rails, il a misé sur l'attrait des couleurs qui rendent les iMac si séduisantes. Lors du Salon de l'électronique grand public de cette année, presque tous les fabricants présentaient des produits aux tons acidulés, une pâle imitation de la palette de couleurs iMac. Si, par le passé, quelques tentatives timides ont été faites pour élargir la gamme de coloris, il semblerait qu'aujourd'hui, tout le monde joue la carte de la couleur: des appareils photo numériques aux téléviseurs en passant par les souris et les claviers. Mais il a d'abord fallu qu'un Steve Jobs annonce justement la couleur et permette d'apporter une touche de gaieté dans le morne quotidien de la vie des bureaux. Et c'est là que réside le génie de Steve Jobs: anticiper l'avenir.

Steve Jobs s'est également chargé de trouver une agence publicitaire, et son choix s'est porté sur Chiat/Day. Jay Chiat bénéficiait d'une longue expérience, avait une grande qualité d'écoute et était un excellent observateur. En outre, il avait suffisamment de persévérance pour tenir tête à Steve Jobs et disposait des ressources créatives nécessaires pour faire de grandes pubs.

Autre point déterminant: Steve Jobs collaborait avec Jay Chiat et l'agence pour élaborer les campagnes publicitaires. Aucun intermédiaire n'intervenait. Evoquant la stratégie publicitaire, Steve Jobs a déclaré: «Nous nous creusons vraiment la cervelle parce que nous voulons toujours faire ce qui est juste et nous voulons le faire bien. Pour nous, le design s'articule autour de quatre aspects: tout d'abord, il y a le graphisme, puis la publicité, ensuite ce qui apparaît à l'écran et enfin, le design du produit lui-même. Et nous pensons que nous sommes des pionniers dans chacun de ces domaines.» (P.-S.: Et ils le sont vraiment.)

Résultat de cette étroite collaboration: le célèbre spot TV «1984». Steve a adoré. Mais Jay Chiat se souvient: «Quand nous avons montré le spot au conseil d'administration d'Apple avant le début du Superbowl, il y a eu un silence gêné. Puis, l'un d'entre eux a demandé: «Est-ce que nous cherchons une nouvelle agence publicitaire?» Le spot n'est passé qu'une fois… durant l'édition 1984 du Superbowl. Le lendemain, les Mac vendus ont atteint, en l'espace de quatre heures seulement, la somme rondelette de 6,5 millions de dollars.» Chiat/Day conserva le budget Apple.

En dépit des difficultés apparemment insurmontables rencontrées par Apple, la société était toujours fermement décidée à conquérir le segment des affaires. IBM s'était imposée auprès des 500 plus grandes entreprises, si bien qu'une pénétration du marché semblait impossible. Steve Hayden explique: «Puis nous avons produit le spot des Lemmings – le successeur de «1984» … un sacré défi. On nous a parlé de bars bruyants où l'on entendait une mouche voler dès que le spot passait... Et, à la fin du spot, un tonnerre d'applaudissements venait rompre ce silence.»

Lorsque les ventes d'Apple décollèrent également à l'étranger, des changements s'imposèrent au niveau de la publicité, mais Chiat/Day manqua le coche. L'équipe de l'agence était démoralisée et morose; ils ne pouvaient pas croire qu'Apple allait les lâcher après des années de collaboration fructueuse. Mais lorsque Steve Jobs retourna chez Apple pour le deuxième round, il rappela aussitôt Lee Clow et Chiat/Day. Ceux-ci ne tardèrent pas à concevoir la désormais célèbre campagne *Think Different*. Fallait-il remercier Lee? Ou Jobs? Ou était-ce l'œuvre de Lee et celle de Jobs, qui pensaient à leur façon au problème d'Apple?

Think Different, c'est de la publicité à l'état pur. Pas une virgule inutile. Pas de papier glacé multicolore. Ce type de publicités n'a aucune chance face à l'effet hypnotique produit par les idées rebelles des grands penseurs de la pub, qui se traduisent en métaphores visuelles à même de perpétuer la vision originale et unique de Macintosh. Le monde de la pub devrait en prendre note: malgré toutes les campagnes, toutes les annonces presse et tout le cirque que l'on fait pour vendre un produit, on peut encore créer de grandes publicités. Jay Chiat l'a prouvé. Et Lee Clow en est toujours capable.

Qu'ajouter de plus? Un client qui inspire. Une agence exceptionnelle qui livre des publicités étonnantes dont la plupart des agences ne peuvent que rêver. «C'est presque effrayant de voir comment Steve peut critiquer une pub et accorder autant d'importance à l'argent. Je suis sûr qu'il est le directeur artistique le mieux payé des Etats-Unis», a déclaré Tom Hughes, directeur créatif d'Apple. Merci Lee. Et, surtout, merci Steve Jobs. Et pour le dire avec les mots de Steve Jobs: «Insanely great!»

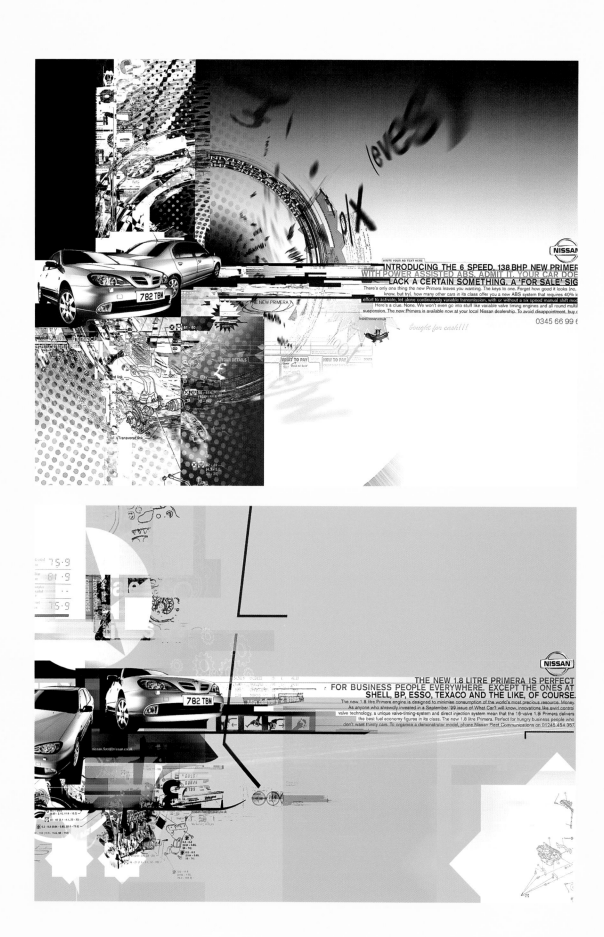

Agency: TBWA Art Director: Paul Belford Creative Director: Trevor Beattie Designer: Dan Beckett, Paul Belford Photographer: Graham Ford, Laurie Haskell, Paul Belford Copywriter: Nigel Roberts
Client: Nissan Motor GB

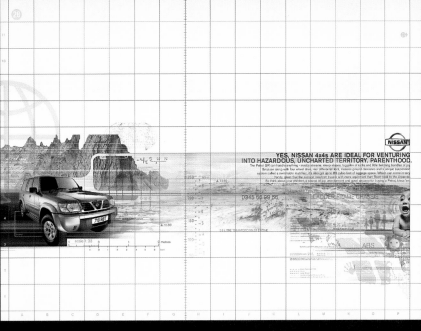

YES, NISSAN 4x4s ARE IDEAL FOR VENTURING
INTO HAZARDOUS, UNCHARTED TERRITORY. PARENTHOOD.

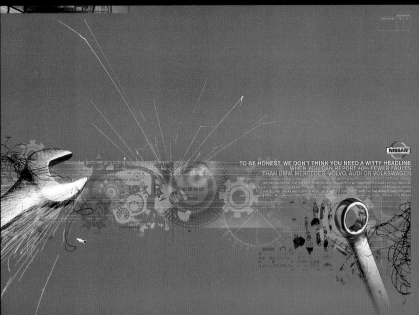

TO BE HONEST, WE DON'T THINK YOU NEED A WITTY HEADLINE
WHEN YOU CAN REPORT 40% FEWER FAULTS
THAN BMW, MERCEDES, VOLVO, AUDI OR VOLKSWAGEN.

NORMALLY, LASTING 24 HOURS ISN'T MUCH OF A RELIABILITY
CLAIM. UNLESS, OF COURSE, THE WORDS
'LE' AND 'MANS' HAPPEN TO BE IN THE SAME SENTENCE.

Title: **FILLER CAP**
ARTIST: *Freeman Thomas*
FORMAT: *Audi TT Coupe*
MEDIUM: *Aluminium*

Title: **AIR VENT**
ARTIST: *Romulus Rost*
FORMAT: *Audi TT Coupe*
MEDIUM: *Aluminium, carbon polymers*

TITLE: **GEAR SHIFT**

ARTIST: Romulus Rost
FORMAT: Audi TT Coupe
MEDIUM: Aluminum, rubber, steel

Agency: Fallon McElligott Art Director: Steve Sage Creative Director: David Lubars Photographer: Mark LaFavor Copywriter: Joe Sweet Client: BMW

Agency: Fallon McElligott Art Director: David Carter Creative Director: David Lubars Photographer: Clint Clemens Copywriter: Joe Sweet Client: BMW

UPGRADE YOUR DRIVE.

THE ELECTRIC CAR IS HERE.

gmev.com

FASTER THAN A SPEEDING ELECTRON.

THE ELECTRIC CAR IS HERE.

gmev.com

Agency: Publicis & Hal Riney Art Director: Mike Mazza Creative Director: Mike Mazza Photographer: R.J. Muna Copywriter: Jack Harding Client: EVI (General Motors)

Agency: Ad Agency Art Director: Toygar Bazarkaya, Erh Ray Creative Director: Steven Landsberg Designer: Toygar Bazarkaya Photographer: Jeff Offenbach Copywriter: Dan Cohen, Stewart Krull Client: Bentley

109 reasons to choose a Dodge Caravan.
Not one of which, believe it or not, involves having kids.

1. We're the folks who invented the minivan. We've initiated pretty much every major design innovation. Have you ever known a copy to be better than the original?

2. Grocery bag hooks on the rear bench seat. Hey, we know it's just a little thing, but if we put this much thought into the details, imagine how much we worry about the big stuff.

3. Made in Canada, of course.

4. Choose between long wheel base or short.

5. Let the store put that bike together for you. Space is no longer a problem.

6. Dual sliding doors. We invented 'em. The other guys are busy catching up.

7. Tubular steel side-guard door beams.

8. Doing a little home reno? Imagine what you could do with up to 168.5 cu.ft. of carrying capacity. Try fitting a 4X8 sheet of drywall or a bunch of 2X4s into that sporty little 2-seater you were looking at.

9. Dodge Caravans really do drive like a car. We know-if you've never driven one, it's hard to believe, but don't take our word on it. Take one for a test drive.

10. Need a place to change at the beach? We modestly suggest a Caravan.

11. Optional built-in child seats.

12. Optional high-output 3.8 litre OHV SMPI V6 engine for 180 horsepower and 240 ft-lb of torque. Does that sound like soccer-mom territory to you?

13. Winner of Carguide's "Best Buy" award for 1999."

14. Winner of Carguide's "Best Buy" award for 1998."

15. Winner of Carguide's "Best Buy" award for 1997."

16. Winner of Carguide's "Best Buy" award for 1995."

17. ...okay, so you get the general idea with the awards. If we listed them all, we'd probably need another page. Let's just say it's the most awarded minivan in history.

18. It's been the best-selling minivan in Canada for 15 years. Which, perhaps coincidentally, is the same amount of time there have been minivans in Canada.

19. Next-Generation, reduced-impact airbags are standard on all models.

20. Available all-wheel-drive on three separate models.

21. Power door locks.

22. Seating for 7 adults. Try that in a so-called luxury car.

23. Room for your golf clubs. Matter of fact, there's probably enough room for an electric cart as well.

24. CFC-free air conditioning.

25. Roof luggage rack. On the highly-unlikely chance that the interior isn't quite big enough. What's more likely is that it's been filled with all your other stuff.

26. Lockable underseat storage.

27. Up to 14 cup or juice box holders. If we put in any more, we'd have to include a bathroom too.

28. And the front one even includes a change holder.

29. Tinted glass and Solar-Control windshield help reduce the greenhouse effect on sunny days.

30. Anti-chip primer on the entire vehicle provides protection from road debris.

31. Things a little cramped at the cottage? Toss a futon or sleeping bag in the back, and presto, an extra room.

32. You know that dog you always wanted for the kids? Make it a Great Dane. Heck, make it two Great Danes.

33. Delivery charges for appliances, furniture, things like that? Kiss 'em good-bye.

34. Power side mirrors.

35. Dual-zone temperature controls.

36. An auxiliary power outlet for your phone or laptop.

37. The view. Sitting up high, you can see the traffic ahead, you can see problems ahead, and you can make sure that problems ahead don't become your problems.

38. Are you a gardener? You can fit a lot of, ah, fertilizer into one of these things.

39. Integrated child seats available.

40. Contractor or tradesperson? A minivan can hold pretty much everything a truck can, and it's covered and locked up.

41. 3-year/60,000 km warranty.

42. Actually, ignore the warranty for a second. Just take a look around. How many old Dodge Caravans do you see on the road, compared to other minivans? Exactly.

43. Cab-forward design gives more interior space.

44. Rear-seat headrests are standard on all models.

45. Windshield wiper electric de-icer.

46. Sporting types take note. Short of yachting, you can fit in pretty much any equipment you'll need.

47. An incredibly tight turning radius.

48. Not to brag or anything, but Caravan has been a Consumer's Digest Best Buy for 10 years in a row.

49. Unibody construction, for a lightweight but strong frame.

50. Fully-independent front suspension.

51. Fold-down rear seats.

52. Okay, if folding down the seats isn't enough, just take them out. Easy Out™ Roller Seats make it a snap.

53. AM/FM cassette stereo is standard, or you can step up to an in-dash CD player.

54. Child-protection locks are standard.

55. Optional Captain Seats in the centre row recline or fold flat to provide a handy tray/table area.

56. Forget to lock your doors before heading out? Caravan automatically takes care of it once you hit 25km/hr.

57. Getting married? Move the whole bridal party in one vehicle.

58. Shoulder-belt height adjusters.

59. Another little thing. There's a small arrow near the fuel gauge to remind you which side of the vehicle to bring up to the gas pump.

60. Sliding doors lock in the open position to keep them from accidentally closing.

61. Remote keyless entry with panic alarm.

62. Low-speed traction control limits wheelspin when conditions are slippery.

63. Power-assisted rack and pinion steering translates into precise, responsive handling.

64. Convenient lights in the liftgate make loading up after dark just a little easier.

65. Standard electric rear defroster.

66. Dual foldaway side mirrors keep you looking good in car washes and other tight spots.

67. Standard tilt steering column accommodates all the drivers in your family.

68. As does the optional eight-way power driver's seat.

69. Not just a light warning for low fuel-it also chimes. Just one more little thing, but they start to add up, don't they?

70. Do you do some of your own maintenance? Well-marked yellow service points under the hood make it way easier.

71. Those aren't just arm rests in the back. Lift them up and they're deep storage bins.

72. Or if you like things even handier, a cargo net between the front seats puts whatever you want right at your fingertips.

73. Ever been in a situation where the sun just sneaks around the visor? Now both visors can be extended.

74. You know that great armoire you found at a great price at the yard sale? Now you can get it home.

75. The Caravan's Enhanced Accident Response System turns on interior lights and automatically unlocks doors (if equipped with power door locks) after air bag deployment if the electrical system remains intact.

76. Tend to forget and leave the lights on? A battery saver feature automatically turns off any lights that are accidentally left on.

77. Even with the third seat in place, the Grand Caravan offers 23.7 cu.ft. of storage space.

78. A fuel-door interlock prevents accidental side-door opening when you're refuelling.

79. Planning on doing a lot of driving? You might want to treat yourself to the optional heated, leather-faced front bucket seats. Think living room on wheels.

80. The Mid-Cab Comfort Control makes sure that passengers in the rear stay comfortable too.

81. Maintain stability no matter what you're carrying with a load-levelling rear suspension.

82. Properly equipped, the Caravan can let you haul trailers weighing up to 1,588kg.

83. Steering wheel mounted speed controls, so you can keep your eyes on the road.

84. Automatic dimming driver's-side exterior mirror, so you can reduce glare from following cars.

85. The Caravan's exterior is more aerodynamic than some cars. Which makes for a quieter ride and better mileage.

86. Damage-resistant, rust-proof plastic full wheel covers.

87. Even the rear washer/wiper has a delay feature.

88. Autostick™ on the Grand Caravan ES lets you choose the ease of an automatic or the added control of clutchless manual shifting.

89. Centre and rear bench seat can fold forward or backward for extra versatility.

90. Having a party? Pick up everything you need-food, refreshments, extra lampshades-all in one trip.

91. Long boards are no problem. Under-seat clearance allows unobstructed clearance for long objects.

92. Going skiing? See #91.

93. The spare tire's mounted under the rear of the vehicle, easily accessed with a built-in winch system.

94. Vehicle theft alarm, including a panic button for extra security.

95. A wide walk-through area between the front seats offers easy access to the rear of the vehicle. But please remain seated until the vehicle has come to a complete stop and the captain has turned the seatbelt sign off.

96. Simple, easy to read analogue instrument panel.

97. Heated exterior rearview mirrors melt away ice and snow. Hey, this is Canada.

98. The Homelink™ Universal Transceiver. It can control garage door openers from the driver's seat, and is one of the few opportunities for the fairer sex to actually handle the remote control.

99. Standard front-wheel drive gives excellent stability and steering control, along with enhanced traction.

100. You can remove the centre bench and move the rear seat up to create limousine seating for middle row passengers.

101. Got a lot of packing to do? Interior lights can be turned off with the flick of a switch to save the battery when you're loading.

102. Overhead console features a trip computer that displays temperature, direction, distance, and more.

103. That same console also has room for your sunglasses.

104. There's a handle on the back of each front seat. Again, a little thing, but they sure make getting in and out easier.

105. Standard front windshield electric de-icer. See Canada remark from #97.

106. Capacity for at least a week's worth of groceries. Probably a year's worth if you don't have teenagers.

107. Rained out while camping? The Caravan also makes a very cosy tent.

108. Adjustable armrests on the front bucket seats.

109. The last reason? Why don't you tell us? You can reach us on the web at www.daimlerchrysler.ca or call us at 1-800-361-3700. Maybe there are another 109 reasons out there.

Dodge Caravan ⬥ Canada's best selling minivan.

(top) Agency: BBDO Canada Creative Director: Michael McLaughlin, Jack Neary Photographer: Terry Collier Copywriter: Neil Murchison Client: Daimler Chrysler *(middle)* Agency: BBDO Canada Art Director: Ken Morgan Creative Director: Michael McLaughlin, Jack Neary Photographer: Terry Collier Copywriter: Neil Murchison Client: Daimler Chrysler *(bottom)* Agency: BBDO Canada Art Director: Ken Morgan Creative Director: Michael McLaughlin, Jack Neary Photographer: Terry Collier Copywriter: Neil Murchison Client: Daimler Chrysler

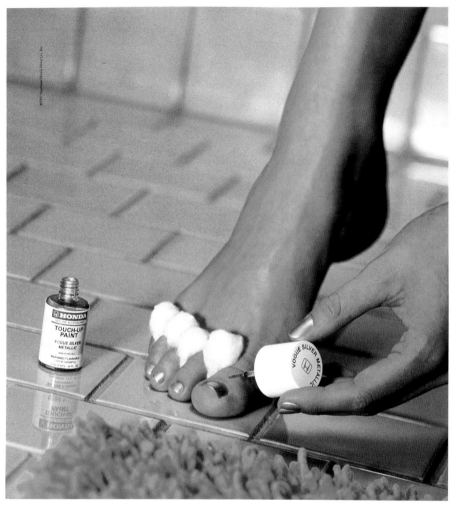

The Civic Coupe

The Civic Coupe

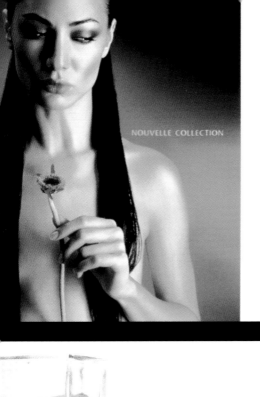

NOUVELLE COLLECTION

TWINGO. DIE NEUE COLLECTION. VERRÜCKTER DENN JE.

TWINGO. DIE NEUE COLLECTION. VERRÜCKTER DENN JE

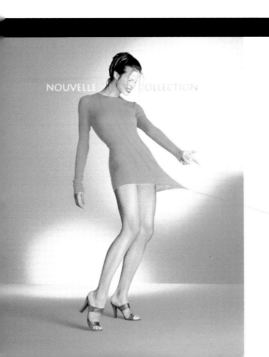

NOUVELLE COLLECTION

TWINGO. DIE NEUE COLLECTION. VERRÜCKTER DENN JE.

NEVER

The new 250 hp S4 · Blistering 2.7 liter, biturbo, 30-valve V6 · Full-time quattro® all-wheel drive · Choice of 6-speed manual or 5-speed Tiptronic® automatic transmission · Zero to 60 in 5.9 seconds · You'll never want to slow down, let alone stop · www.audiusa.com

TAKE EVERY

The A6 Avant · 200 hp V6 · 5-valve engine technology · Full-time quattro® all-wheel drive · 5-speed Tiptronic® automatic transmission · Over 73 cubic feet of cargo space · A car that follows your heart wherever it goes · www.audiusa.com

The new A8 4.2 · Thundering 300 hp V8 · Race-bred 5-valve engine technology · Full-time quattro® all-wheel drive · 5-speed Tiptronic® automatic transmission · Flared fenders, lower stance, muscular profile · Bliss begins in second gear · www.audiusa.com

Agency: Ammirati Puris Lintas Art Director: Vancelee Teng Creative Director: Nick Fairhead Photographer: Mun's Studio Illustrator: Pro Colour Copywriter: Justin Pereira Client: Audi Asia Pacific

Man's reach should exceed his grasp. Such is the spirit that drives Audi. A feeling that nothing is impossible. That the future of roadholding may take a new turn. Those who have experienced quattro need no convincing.

[Roadholding]

You can't forge ahead by sticking to existing routes.

The aim of technology is to ultimately improve the quality of life. At Audi to improve means to explore virtually every possibility. There's no telling where a shift in thinking might lead.

[Future]

There are no limits to the mind.

Agency: McKinney&Silver Art Director: Bob Ranew Creative Director: David Baldwin Designer: Kathy Jerrett Photographer: Jim Erickson Copywriter: Christopher Wilson Client: Audi of America

How to gently prepare yourself for the inevitable fate of the BMW Z8 in James Bond's new movie.

(Please fold slowly.)

FOLD HERE

The new BMW Z8.

www.bmw.com

Freude am Fahren

"Aaaaaaaaaaargh."

Chris Bangle,
BMW Director of Design

Dented in Scene 42.

Torn in Scene 148.

Totaled in Scene 391.

Scratched in Scene 94.

Punctured in Scene 212.

Crushed in Scene 68.

The new BMW Z8 as seen in "The World Is Not Enough."

The new BMW Z8.

www.bmw.com

Freude am Fahren

Agency: Fallon McElligott Art Director: Bob Barrie Creative Director: David Lubars Designer: Bob Barrie Photographer: Mark LaFavor Copywriter: Tom Rosen Client: BMW

Agency: Fallon McElligott Art Director: Tom Lichtenheld Creative Director: David Lubars Photographer: Nicolas Pavlov, Mark LaFavor Copywriter: Mike Gibbs, Riley Kane Client: BMW

(top) Agency: GSD&M Art Director: David Crawford Creative Director: David Crawford, Rich Terry Photographer: George Simoni Copywriter: Cameron Day Client: Roger Beasley Porsche
(bottom) Agency: GSD&M Art Director: David Crawford Creative Director: David Crawford, Rich Terry Photographer: George Simoni Copywriter: Rich Terry Client: Roger Beasley Porsche

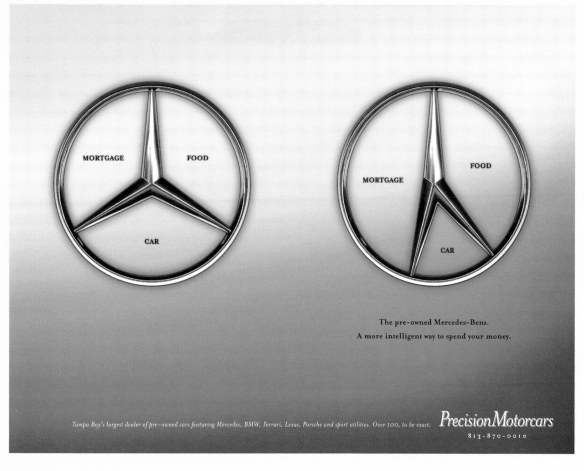

(top) Agency: GSD&M Art Director: Brett Stiles Creative Director: David Crawford, Cameron Day Photographer: Scott Harben Copywriter: Russell Lambrecht Client: Pennzoil Quaker State Corp. *(bottom)*
Agency: Fahlgren/Tampa Art Director: John Stapleton Creative Director: Scott Sheinberg Photographer: John Stapleton Copywriter: James Rosene Client: Precision Motorcars

Agency: EganStJames Art Director: Eddie Choi Creative Director: Lee St. James Photographer: Tim Damon, Craig Guyon Copywriter: Larry Werner Client: Eaton Corp., Dana Corp.

People drooling over your car. It may not be pretty, but it's a problem we'd all like to have. That's why there's Classic.® It has the highest concentration of carnauba among the leading waxes. So your car gets a deep, rich shine with unparalleled protection every time. Since 1952, for a really great wax there's always been Classic.

CLASSIC NOT ONLY GIVES YOUR CAR A DEEP, RICH SHINE, IT ALSO PROTECTS AGAINST UNSIGHTLY DROOL.

Classic

LOVE. HONOR. POLISH.™

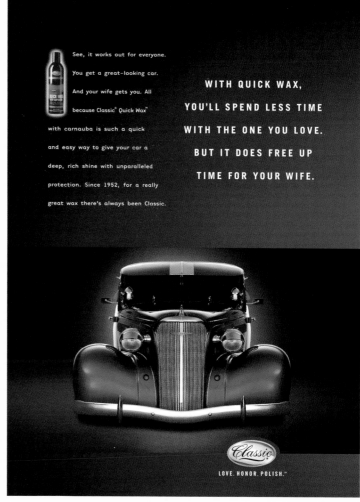

See, it works out for everyone. You get a great-looking car. And your wife gets you. All because Classic® Quick Wax® with carnauba is such a quick and easy way to give your car a deep, rich shine with unparalleled protection. Since 1952, for a really great wax there's always been Classic.

WITH QUICK WAX, YOU'LL SPEND LESS TIME WITH THE ONE YOU LOVE. BUT IT DOES FREE UP TIME FOR YOUR WIFE.

Classic

LOVE. HONOR. POLISH.™

Agency: GSD&M Art Director: Brett Stiles Creative Director: David Crawford, Rich Terry Photographer: R.J. Muna Copywriter: Tom Campion Client: Pennzoil Quaker State Corp.

Frank Sinatra

1915-1998

It was a great ride.

Cadillac.

Agency: The Campaign Palace Creative Director: Richard Hollingum Photographer: Gary Heery Copywriter: John McCabe Client: Land Rover

Agency: Work Art Director: Mike Boulia Creative Director: David Waraksa, Cabell Harris Designer: David Waraksa Photographer: Heather Fleinor Copywriter: Anne Marie Floyd Client: Kendall Jackson Winery

Agency: Work Art Director: Mike Boulia Creative Director: David Waraksa, Cabell Harris Designer: David Waraksa Photographer: Tonya Boulia Copywriter: Anne Marie Floyd Client: Kendall Jackson Winery

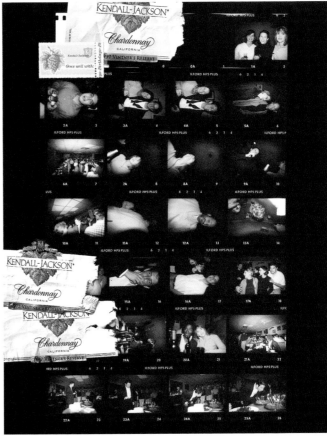

Agency: Work Art Director: Mike Boulia Creative Director: Cabell Harris Designer: David Waraksa Photographer: Abe Spear Copywriter: Anne Marie Floyd Client: Kendall Jackson Winery

Agency: Work Art Director: Mike Boulia Creative Director: Cabell Harris Designer: David Waraksa Photographer: Cabell Harris Copywriter: Anne Marie Floyd Client: Kendall Jackson Winery

LIFT WITH YOUR LEGS

THIS SPACE FOR OFFICE USE ONLY

MFG. BY MAIN ST BEER CO • 1911 W MAIN ST • RICHMOND VA USA

CLOCK OUT | POP A TOP | FOR A JOB WELL DONE

MONDAY TUESDAY WEDNESDAY THURSDAY FRIDAY SATURDAY SUNDAY

AM 1 2 3 4 5 6 7 8 9 10 11 12 PM 1 2 3 4 5 6 7 8 9 10 11 12

WORK BEER CONTAINER CATEGORY:

bottle 6-pak case keg ▲

WORK
1,968 Fluid Ounces | BEER

WORK BEER FACTS
The Bureau of Labor Statistics reports over 30,000 hernia cases a year. 93% occur in men. Hernias are common in nurses and orderlies whose job requires lifting patients, and butchers who carry large hunks of meat. Average work days lost due to hernia: 21.

Note: June is National Hernia Month.

Agency: Work Art Director: David Waraksa, Cabell Harris Creative Director: Cabell Harris Photographer: Karl Steinbrenner Client: Work Beer

FOR A JOB WELL DONE

WORK
12 Fluid Ounces
(335ml)
BEER

WORK BEER FACTS
A novice hand model is usually paid around
$70 an hour, while a professional hand model
with a national reputation can earn up to
$250 an hour.

The person in this ad is not a professional
hand model. He is a brick mason.

THIS SPACE FOR OFFICE USE ONLY

MFG. BY MAIN ST. BEER CO. • 1911 W. MAIN ST. • RICHMOND VA USA

WORK BEER CONTAINER CATEGORY:

bottle 6-pak case keg

CLOCK OUT | POP A TOP | YOU EARNED IT

MONDAY TUESDAY WEDNESDAY THURSDAY FRIDAY SATURDAY SUNDAY

AM 1 2 3 4 5 6 7 8 9 10 11 12 | 1 2 3 4 5 6 7 8 9 10 11 12 PM

Agency: Clarity Coverdale Fury Art Director: Jac Coverdale Creative Director: Jac Coverdale Photographer: Raymond Meeks Copywriter: Jerry Fury Client: Belvedere Vodka

L'ABUS D'ALCOOL EST DANGEREUX POUR LA SANTE, CONSOMMEZ AVEC MODERATION.

L'ABUS D'ALCOOL EST DANGEREUX POUR LA SANTE, CONSOMMEZ AVEC MODERATION.

L'ABUS D'ALCOOL EST DANGEREUX POUR LA SANTE, CONSOMMEZ AVEC MODERATION.

L'ABUS D'ALCOOL EST DANGEREUX POUR LA SANTE, CONSOMMEZ AVEC MODERATION.

MAIN ST. BEER CO.

BEER CLUB APPLICATION

ARE YOU 21 YEARS OR OLDER?   YES_____   NO_____

Return completed application to Main Street Beer Company, 1911 West Main Street. All new members will be issued a membership card and a handsome certificate suitable for framing.

OFFICE USE ONLY

APPROVED ☐   DENIED ☐

NAME   DATE

MAIN ST. BEER CO.
1911 W. Main St. • Richmond, VA • 23220

Agency: Fallon McElligott Art Director: Bob Barrie Creative Director: David Lubars Designer: Bob Barrie Photographer: Mark LaFavor Copywriter: Riley Kane Client: Starbucks

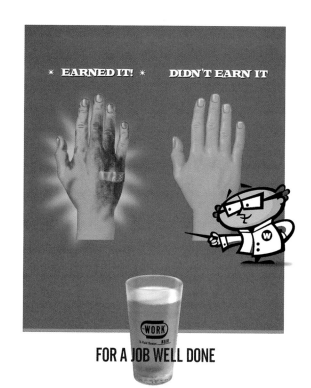

A Good Time Was Had by All

Y
ESTᴰ 1849
YALUMBA
SERIOUSLY AUSTRALIAN

They Have One Thing in Common

Y
ESTᴰ 1849
YALUMBA
SERIOUSLY AUSTRALIAN

You Can Take It With You

Y
ESTᴰ 1849
YALUMBA
SERIOUSLY AUSTRALIAN

Half Full or Half Empty

Y
ESTᴰ 1849
YALUMBA
SERIOUSLY AUSTRALIAN

Agency: SSC&B Lintas Art Director: Mahendra Bhagat Creative Director: Mahendra Bhagat, Amar K. Deb Copywriter: Amar K. Deb Client: UDV Ltd.

FOREVER YOUNG.

FOREVER YOUNG.

Agency: BBDO Canada Art Director: Michael McLaughlin Creative Director: Michael McLaughlin, Jack Neary Photographer: Chris Gordaneer Copywriter: Jack Neary Client: Pepsi-Cola Canada Beverages

(top, left) Agency: Jung von Matt Art Director: Timm Haneback, Katrin Oeding Creative Director: Hartwig Keuntje, Heier Rogge Photographer: Chin Choi, Stephan Försterling Copywriter: Matthias Harbeck Client: Bavaria-St. Pauli-Brauerei GmbH *(top, right)* Agency: Jung von Matt Art Director: Timm Haneback, Katrin Oeding Creative Director: Hartwig Keuntje, Heier Rogge Photographer: Salvatore Vinci, Stephan Försterling Copywriter: Matthias Harbeck Client: Bavaria-St. Pauli-Brauerei GmbH *(bottom)* Agency: Jung von Matt Art Director: Timm Haneback, Katrin Oeding Creative Director: Hartwig Keuntje, Heier Rogge Photographer: Chin Choi, Stephan Försterling Copywriter: Matthias Harbeck Client: Bavaria-St. Pauli-Brauerei GmbH

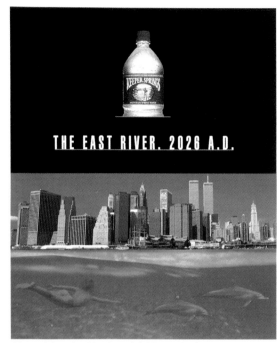

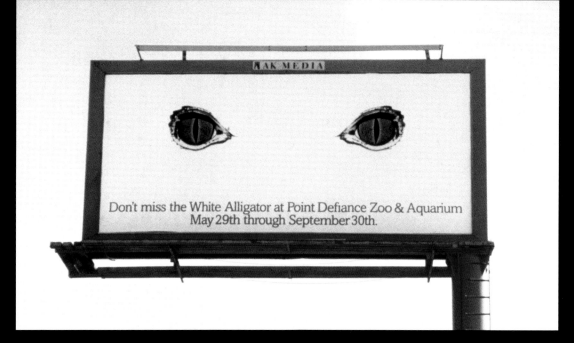

(top) Agency: Wongdoody Art Director: Jason Black Creative Director: Tracy Wong Copywriter: Jeanne Ivy Client: Point Defiance Zoo *(bottom)* Agency: Young & Laramore Art Director: Pam Kelliher Photographer: Tod Martens Illustrator: Jeff Durham Copywriter: Scott Montgomery Client: Red Gold, Inc.

Agency: Di Zinno Thompson Art Director: Rob Petrie Creative Director: Craig Evans Copywriter: Craig Evans Client: San Diego Convention & Visitors Bureau

Agency: Young & Laramore Creative Director: David Young, Jeff Laramore Illustrator: David Bellamy, 2nd Globe Client: Ossip Optometry

Agency: Bailey Lauerman Art Director: Sean Faden Creative Director: Sean Faden Designer: Thomas Irvin Photographer: Rick Neibel Illustrator: Thomas Irvin Copywriter: Nick
Main Client: University of Nebraska Athletic Department

Agency: Fallon McElligott Art Director: Dan Bryant Creative Director: David Lubars Copywriter: Greg Hahn Client: Nikon

Agency: The Richards Group Art Director: Lee Coleman, Dean Oram Creative Director: Stan Richards Photographer: James Schwartz Copywriter: Kevin Paetzel Client: Nokia Mobile Phones

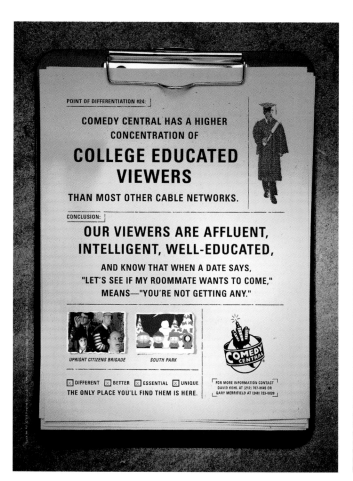

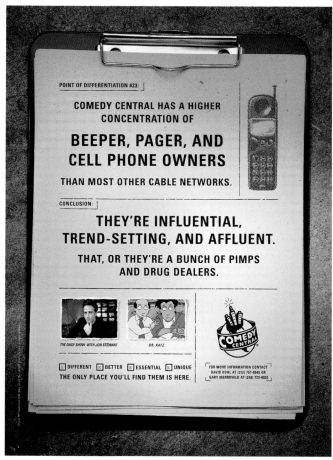

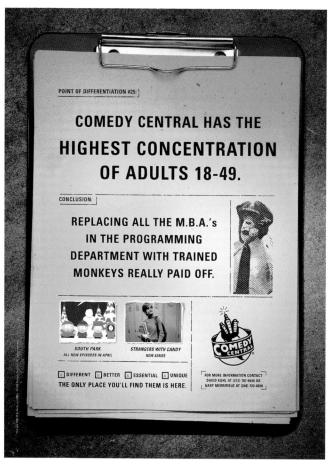

Agency: Butler, Shine & Stern Art Director: Jerome Marruci Creative Director: John Butler, Mike Shine Copywriter: Alex Grossman Client: Comedy Central

Millions of people
can't wait to watch the grass grow.

Or their favorite programs on the network that hits closest to home.   *hgtv.com*

For countless millions,
it's provocative, it's entertaining,
it's thrilling,
it's faucet installation.

And it keeps getting better on the network that brings millions home.   *hgtv.com*

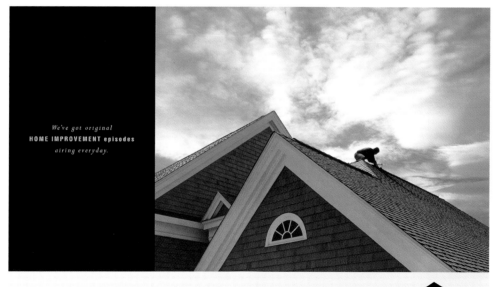

We've got original
HOME IMPROVEMENT episodes
airing everyday.

And all night, too, on the only network that's built around the home.   *hgtv.com*

They won't stop calling.

Three years. Three calls. We congratulate SBC on winning FORTUNE® magazine's World's Most Admired Telecommunications Company for the third year in a row.   GSD&M

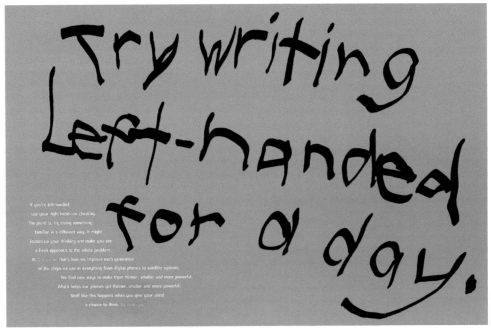

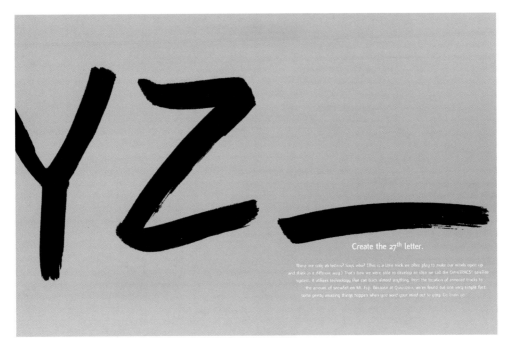

Agency: Fallon McElligott Art Director: Bobby Appleby, Steve Driggs Creative Director: David Lubars Illustrator: Steve Driggs Copywriter: Scott Vincent, Peter McHugh, Linda Birkenstock Client: Qualcomm

When you open people's eyes,
they can't help but remember you.

What makes a great news program? The footage must be gripping. The coverage comprehensive. And the point of view, unmistakably local. That's why we offer a myriad of services and tools that help you make your news truly memorable. For more information, please call 404.827.2340.

Serious about news?

Inside every story,
is a much bigger one.

Nothing grabs a viewer's attention more than news that hits them where they live. So your news must have a local impact. That's why we offer a myriad of resources to help you tailor the kind of stories people can't help but watch. And can never forget. For more information, please call 404.827.2340.

Serious about news?

How can news hit home
and still be 3,000 miles away?

In your world every story has to have a local impact. So whether it's a crisis in Kosovo or a twister in Topeka, we have the resources to let you tailor even far-reaching events to your market's needs. For more information, please call 404.827.2340.

Serious about news?

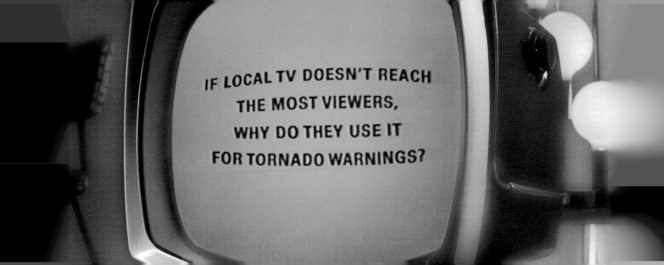

Introducing the Apple Cinema Display. Actual size. Think different.

go

go go

Macworld New York 99 Macworld New York 99 Macworld New Y

More brain. Less brawn.

The New PowerBook G3

Think different.

The Rebirth of Cool.

Think different.

Yum.

Think different.

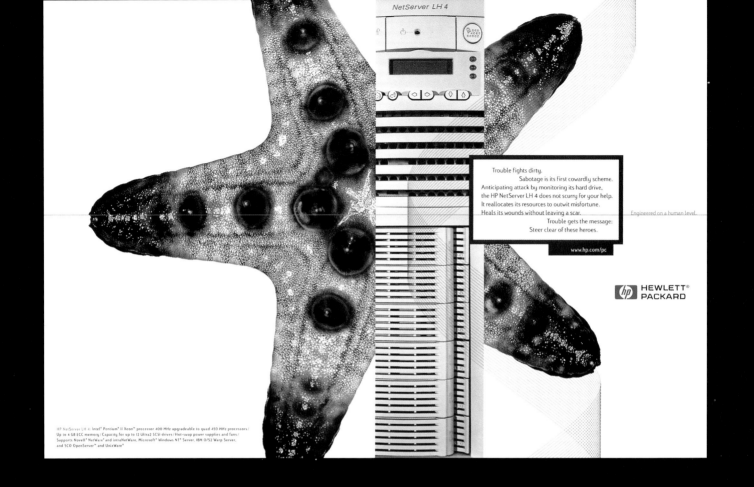

NetServer LH 4

Trouble fights dirty.
Sabotage is its first cowardly scheme.
Anticipating attack by monitoring its hard drive,
the HP NetServer LH 4 does not scurry for your help.
It reallocates its resources to outwit misfortune.
Heals its wounds without leaving a scar.
Trouble gets the message:
Steer clear of these heroes.

Engineered on a human level.

www.hp.com/pc

[hp] HEWLETT®
PACKARD

HP NetServer LH 4: Intel® Pentium® II Xeon™ processor 400 MHz upgradeable to quad 450 MHz processors /
Up to 4 GB ECC memory / Capacity for up to 12 Ultra2 SCSI drives / Hot-swap power supplies and fans /
Supports Novell® NetWare® and intraNetWare, Microsoft® Windows NT® Server, IBM O/S2 Warp Server,
and SCO OpenServer™ and UnixWare®

Heat. Vibration. Shock. Gravity.
All conspire to destroy the things that stand in their wa
Every PC we make is tested against these forces of natur
For our notebooks, it's merely preparation
to do battle with the most malicious menace of all:
the roa

www.hp.com/pc

HP OmniBook XE. Intel® Mobile Pentium® II processor 266PE MHz to 333 MHz or Intel Celeron™ processor 2

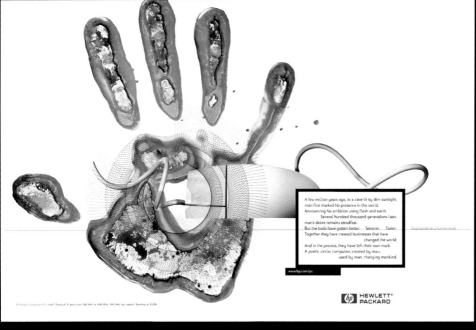
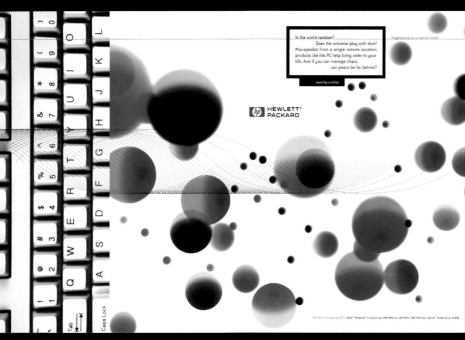
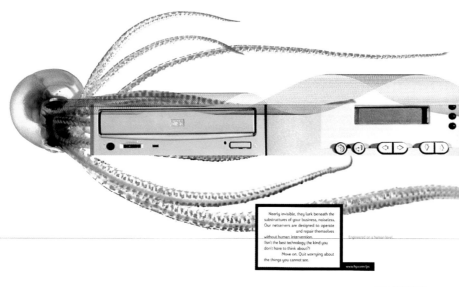

An event is detected.

Failure attacks.

Reacting swiftly, our netserver analyzes the situation and renders a paralyzing block to the bad sector.

Peace is restored.

The republic of your network remains intact.

Engineered on a human level.

www.hp.com/pc

HEWLETT® PACKARD

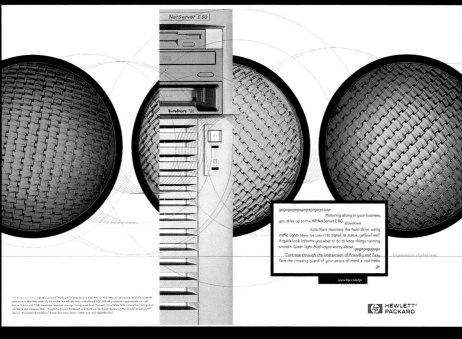

gogogogogogogogogogogostop

Motoring along in your business, you drive up to the HP NetServer E 60. *slowdown*

Auto Alert monitors the hard drive, using traffic lights (those fast talkers) to signal its status. *yellow? red?* A quick look informs you what to do to keep things running smooth. Green light. Nothing to worry about. *gogogogogogo*

Continue through the intersection of Friendly and Easy. Give the crossing guard of your peace of mind a nod hello.

go

Engineered on a human level.

www.hp.com/pc

HEWLETT® PACKARD

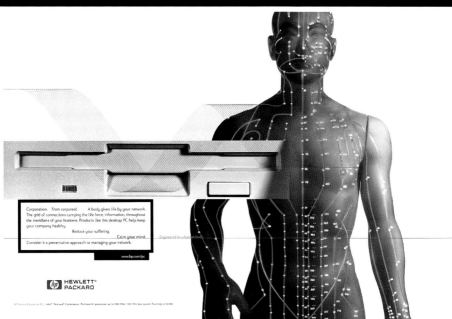

Corporation. From *corporal*. A body given life by your network. The grid of connections carrying the life force, information, throughout the meridians of your business. Products like this desktop PC help keep your company healthy.

Reduce your suffering.

Calm your mind. Engineered on a human level.

Consider it a preventative approach to managing your network.

www.hp.com/pc

HEWLETT® PACKARD

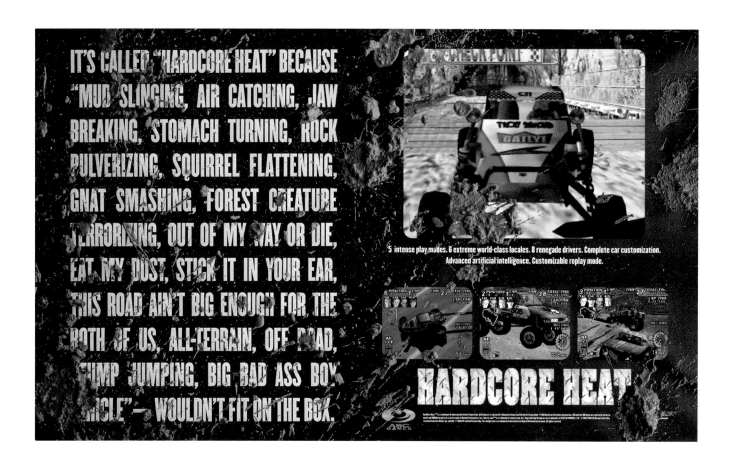

Agency: Work Art Director: Mike Boulia Creative Director: Cabell Harris Designer: Pat Sanavely Copywriter: Anne Marie Floyd Client: ASC Games

The explosion is seventeen minutes away. A gasket is about

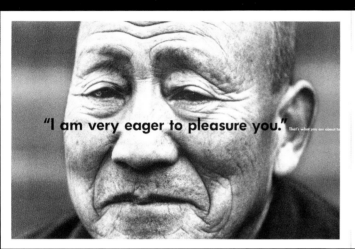

"I am very eager to pleasure you." That's what you are about to

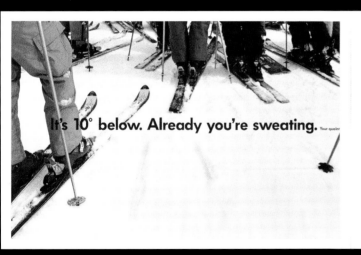

It's 10° below. Already you're sweating. Your quaint

You're dying in Baltimore. Oddly enough, you're killing

Agency: Saatchi & Saatchi, San Francisco Art Director: Joe Kayser, Curtis Melville Creative Director: Curtis Melville, Steve Silver
Photographer: Robert Mizano Copywriter: Rob Jamieson, Russ Lamoureux, Steve Silver Client: Hewlett Packard

Remember, if you get the wind knocked out of you,
stay down so I can examine the color of your face.

Guess you could say we like to go out of our way to make sure stuff looks real.
Why? Because we can. Our 3D graphics accelerator performs over 100 billion operations a second.
And considering our chip is compatible with a ton of games and software, maybe it's time to upgrade
your present computer with a 3dfx Voodoo3™ board, or make sure it's built into your next one.
For more information, check out our website at www.3dfx.com. **So powerful, it's kind of ridiculous.**

3dfx

If it were up to us, every experience would be more intense. Our 3D graphics boards are designed to, shall
we say, heighten things. So whether it's an application for business, home or entertainment, we won't be satisfied until
your senses cry uncle. And with our accelerators performing over 100 billion operations per second, we'll make
damn sure that they do. For more information, check out www.3dfx.com. **So powerful, it's kind of ridiculous.**   **3dfx**

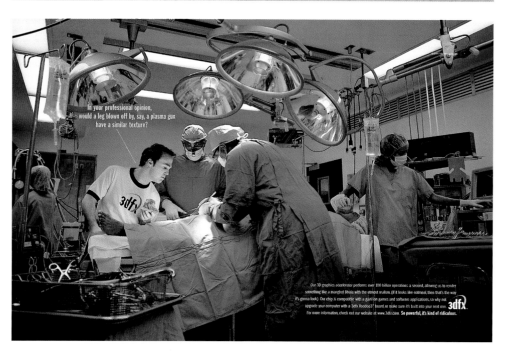

In your professional opinion,
would a leg blown off by, say, a plasma gun
have a similar texture?

Our 3D graphics accelerator performs over 100 billion operations a second, allowing us to render
something like a mangled fibula with the utmost realism. (If it looks like oatmeal, then that's the way
it's gonna look.) Our chip is compatible with a gazillion games and software applications, so why not
upgrade your computer with a 3dfx Voodoo3™ board, or make sure it's built into your next one.   **3dfx**
For more information, check out our website at www.3dfx.com. **So powerful, it's kind of ridiculous.**

(Opposite, top) Agency: Goodby, Silverstein & Partners Art Director: Terry Finley Creative Director: Jeffrey Goodby, Rich Siliverstein Photographer: Shawn Michienzi Copywriter: Matt Smuckler Client: 3dfx *(middle)* Agency: Goodby, Silverstein & Partners Art Director: Melanie Menkemeller Creative Director: Jeffrey Goodby, Rich Siliverstein Photographer: Shawn Michienzi Copywriter: Colin Nissan Client: 3dfx *(bottom)* Agency: Goodby, Silverstein & Partners Art Director: Terry Finley Creative Director: Jeffrey Goodby, Rich Siliverstein Photographer: Shawn Michienzi Copywriter: Matt Smuckler Client: 3dfx

Agency: Ad Agency Art Director: Mark Mueller Creative Director: Mark Mueller, David Perris Illustrator: Hugh Syme Copywriter: David Perris Client: Lockheed Martin

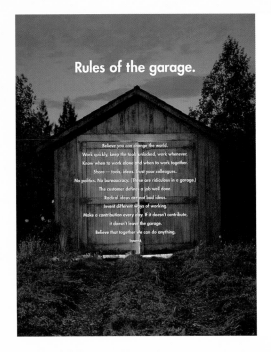

Rules of the garage.

Believe you can change the world.
Work quickly, keep the tools unlocked, work whenever.
Know when to work alone and when to work together.
Share — tools, ideas. Trust your colleagues.
No politics. No bureaucracy. (These are ridiculous in a garage.)
The customer defines a job well done.
Radical ideas are not bad ideas.
Invent different ways of working.
Make a contribution every day. If it doesn't contribute,
it doesn't leave the garage.
Believe that together we can do anything.
Invent.

The original company of inventors started here.

It is returning here.

The original start-up will act like one again.

From this day forward.

www.hp.com

All kids are inventors.

It's because they're not afraid
to get their hands filthy.
To eat the paste.
To use a hammer as a brush.
To break something just to see how it works.
And to start with the impossible,
which is where grownups usually stop.
Just a few of the things we're keeping in mind
as we invent the new hp.
Want to come along?
www.hp.com

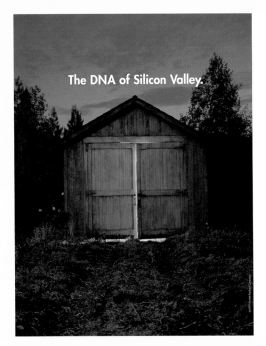

The DNA of Silicon Valley.

The original company of inventors started here.
367 Addison Avenue, the garage out back.
Two young inventors, radicals really,
with a few simple tools and a passion to invent.
In this garage more than a company was born.
The spirit that has launched hundreds of companies was born.
Now the original company of inventors is returning here,
to this garage, to that spirit.

The original start-up
will act like one again. Watch.
www.hp.com

Agency: Goodby, Silverstein & Partners Art Director: Mark Winneker Creative Director: Jeffrey Goodby, Rich Silverstein Photographer: Robert Mizano Copywriter: Dante Lombardi Client: Hewlett Packard

HARDENED BY EXPERIENCE.

It's no coincidence that the biggest name in laminates for thirty years, makes the longest-lasting, hardest-wearing range. Every piece is designed to take scratches, spills and knocks, year after year, without showing its age. Formica laminates - made durable enough to stand the test of time.

30 YEARS AND STILL FRESH.

How do you stay fresh for thirty years? Ask Formica. After all, it has been the leading name in laminates for decades. New, trend-setting colours, styles and textures are still delivered with the Formica quality you trust. Whatever comes next, it won't be old age.

IT'S ALWAYS HAND-PICKED.

A Formica laminate gets attention even before the outside world lays eyes on it. From the moment a design is selected, till it's ready to be sold, it is repeatedly tested to make sure it lives up to the Formica name. It always does. So, no matter which Formica you eventually choose, we can assure you it's perfect.

Agency: SSC&B Lintas Art Director: Umesh Bhagat Copywriter: Monish Dayal Client: Bombay Burmah Trading Co.

The stars have aligned.

Everything falls into place. And suddenly, you find that you're building and strengthening the connection between you and your customers like never before. Karma? Kismet? Actually, it's a much more potent force. It's the power of a pioneer and innovator of customer relationship management since 1973.
Call 1.800.OUTSOURCE and discover the phenomenon called APAC Customer Services. It will do wonders for the shape of your business.

APAC
Customer Services

APAC Customer Services, One Parkway North Center, Deerfield, IL 60015   **1-800-OUTSOURCE**   www.apaccustomerservices.com

The Missing Link.

What will it take to bridge the gap between you and your customers? To build and strengthen the link? It's no mystery. Just connect with the power of a pioneer and innovator of customer relationship management since 1973. Call 1.800.OUTSOURCE and discover the phenomenon called APAC Customer Services. It will help you leave an indelible mark on your industry.

APAC
Customer Services

APAC Customer Services, One Parkway North Center, Deerfield, IL 60015   **1-800-OUTSOURCE**   www.apaccustomerservices.com

Agency: Porrevecchio Advertising Art Director: Steve Nelson Creative Director: Steve Nelson Designer: Steve Nelson, Dan Salva Photographer: Mike Radencich Copywriter: Salva Orenick, Jane Wooldrige Client: APAC Customer Service

HEAVY SHIPMENT? WE'RE READY FOR IT.

HEAVY SHIPMENT? WE'RE READY FOR IT.

HEAVY SHIPMENT? WE'RE READY FOR IT.

Agency: DDB Art Director: Gary Alfredson Creative Director: Gary Alfredson Designer: Gary Alfredson Photographer: Carl Vanderschuit Copywriter: Rick Korzeniowski Client: ftd.com

SOME BEFORE YOU
PUSHED BROOMS.

OTHERS PUSHED
FOR CHANGE.

WHAT WILL YOU PUSH?

YOURSELF?

Alverno
COLLEGE
FOR WOMEN

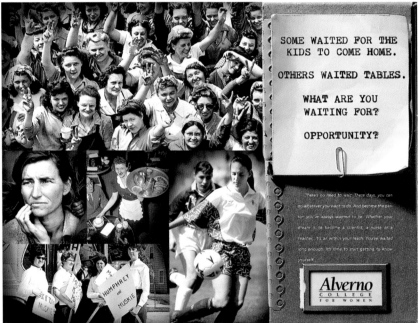

SOME WAITED FOR THE
KIDS TO COME HOME.

OTHERS WAITED TABLES.

WHAT ARE YOU
WAITING FOR?

OPPORTUNITY?

Alverno
COLLEGE
FOR WOMEN

SOME WERE ONLY
GIVEN THE CHANCE
TO APPLY FLOORWAX.

OTHERS, MASCARA.

WHAT WILL YOU APPLY?

YOUR ABILITIES?

Alverno
COLLEGE
FOR WOMEN

Before internship: Mr. Wieden, Mr. Goodby, Mr. Riney.
After internship: Dan, Jeff, Mr. Riney.

How many students do you know who have worked on ESPN with Dan Wieden? Or Miller Lite with Bill Westbrook?

We know three. We also know one more who worked on pitches for Jeff Goodby. And another one who spent this past summer working just down the hall from Gary Goldsmith.

You see, here at the new VCU Adcenter, we have an unusual method of preparing our students for the real world. It's called the real world.

In our first year, we've managed to initiate summer internships with some of the top agencies in the country. Fallon. BBDO. Riney. And, of course, with names like Wieden and Chiat on our board of directors, we also get internships at, well, Wieden and Chiat.

What is it about the VCU Adcenter that has so many good people lining up to help us? For starters, it's not an entirely humanitarian gesture on their part. They know that this is a different kind of ad school. They know that after two years in our program, they'll be looking at a crop of writers, art directors and strategic thinkers who are extremely

hirable. But more importantly, they realize the time has come for ad schools to start preparing students to do more than build spec books. The time has come to give students the foundation they'll need to have long, substantial careers.

Which is precisely why this school was created. Unlike other programs, our writers and art directors are teamed up with account managers and account planners and given real assignments. With the help of full-time professors, strategies are crafted, consumers are interviewed, and your concepts are done and done again, until each one is bulletproof. Ad legends are invited in to lecture on a regular basis. Internships are secured.

In the end, everyone leaves with a smarter book, a master's degree, and a better chance of landing a great job.

Find out more about our unique program for writers, art directors, account managers, account planners and media planners. Call 1-800-311-3341. Or look for us online at www.adcenter.vcu.edu.

And remember, we're not trying to save the world. Just advertising.

VCU Adcenter. Students of Advertising.

We don't mean to name-drop, but (Wieden) our board of (Westbrook) directors is pretty (Dusenberry) impressive.

Did we happen to mention Mike Hughes, the Creative Director of The Martin Agency? Or perhaps Jon Steel, the Director of Planning at Goodby?

We could spend this entire ad listing the names of the ad legends on our board. (And if we have to list their titles, we'll be here all day.) But, to be honest, we'd rather tell you why the current leaders of this industry are helping us build the leaders of the future.

Like us, they took a long, hard look at the current state of advertising and saw juniors floundering without any real guidance. They saw young people discarding rule books they'd never even been asked to read.

Enter the Adcenter at Virginia Commonwealth University. This is not a place where students come to laminate condom ads. The Adcenter was created with loftier goals in mind. Simply put, this is a two-year master's program designed to produce the smartest young writers, art directors and strategic thinkers in the nation.

Or, as Harry Jacobs (yet another of our distinguished board members) put it, "A place where students graduate not just with an amazing portfolio, but the thinking to go along with it."

What makes us so different? For starters, students at the Adcenter are taught by full-time professors, not weekly visitors. They spend two years learning from the nation's best teachers. How to think strategically. How to solve real problems. How to boil mountains of information down into simple, clear, pencil-winning ideas.

The guidance doesn't stop with us, either. We've been able to initiate summer internship programs with blue-chip agencies like Fallon and Wieden (another benefit of all these kahunas on our board). We've even developed a national mentor program where second-year students are "adopted" by industry leaders and given regular feedback.

Everything we do is designed to produce students with real depth, real talent and a real chance of actually having a long, successful career.

Find out more about our unique program for promising young writers, art directors, account managers, account planners and media planners. Call 1-800-311-3341. Or simply look for us online at www.adcenter.vcu.edu.

And remember, we're not trying to save the world. Just advertising.

VCU Adcenter. Students of Advertising.

FEEL THE RAW NAKED POWER OF THE ROAD.

For the bare facts of Jensen's new line of mobile audio systems, visit us at www.jensenaudio.com or call 1(800)67-SOUND.

JENSEN

Agency: Hoffman York Art Director: Ken Butts Creative Director: Tom Jordan Designer: Ken Butts Photographer: Peter Carter Illustrator: Jeff Mueller Copywriter: Tom Jordan Client: Jensen

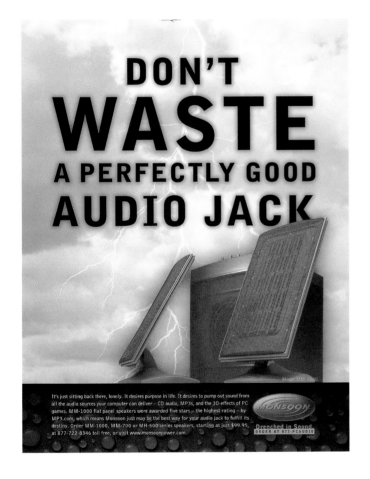

Agency: Young & Laramore Art Director: Mark Bradley Illustrator: Jeff Durham Copywriter: Scott Montgomery Client: Monsoon

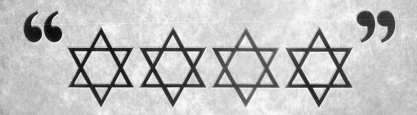

" ✡ ✡ ✡ ✡ "

FIDDLER ON THE ROOF

AUSTIN MUSICAL THEATRE   MAY 4TH THRU 16TH 1999

FOR TICKETS   CALL 469-SHOW

Agency: Work Art Director: David Waraska, Paul Howalt Creative Director: Cabell Harris Designer: Paul Howalt Copywriter: Joe Nagy Client: Work Clothing

Life is short.

Surround yourself with people you can look up to.

Always offer an open hand.

Agency: Fallon McElligott Art Director: Paul Malmström, Kevin Smith Creative Director: David Lubars Designer: Kobe Suvongse Photographer: Veronique Vial Copywriter: Linus Karlsson Client: Lee Europe

DO YOUR BREASTS MAKE YOU UNCOMFORTABLE?

You've hit your stride at what could be a really great run, but there's one problem: your breasts. They're either bouncing so hard it hurts, or they're strapped down by two bras that feel like wet sponges. So you have two choices: run in pain, or wear a bra that's supportive and comfortable. Nike Inner Actives, part of the Nike Alpha Project, are sports bras in real bra sizes. In a new Dri-FIT fabric that won't get soggy. With strategically placed straps and seams that won't dig in or leave big red marks. So if you buy two, it's only because you want a spare. Visit us at **nike.com/inneractives.**

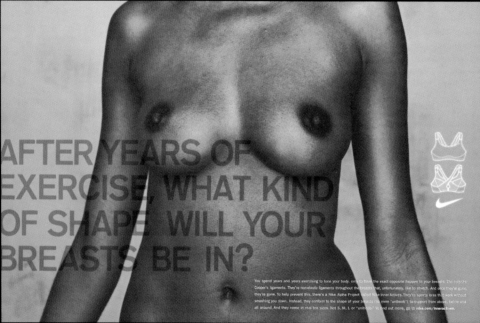

AFTER YEARS OF EXERCISE, WHAT KIND OF SHAPE WILL YOUR BREASTS BE IN?

You spend years and years exercising to tone your body, only to have the exact opposite happen to your breasts. The culprits: Cooper's ligaments. They're non-elastic ligaments throughout the breasts that, unfortunately, like to stretch. And once they're gone, they're gone. To help prevent this, there's a Nike Alpha Project called Nike Inner Actives. They're sports bras that work without smashing you down. Instead, they conform to the shape of your breasts (no more "uniboob") to support from above, below and all around. And they come in real bra sizes. Not S, M, L or "uniboob." To find out more, go to **nike.com/inneractives.**

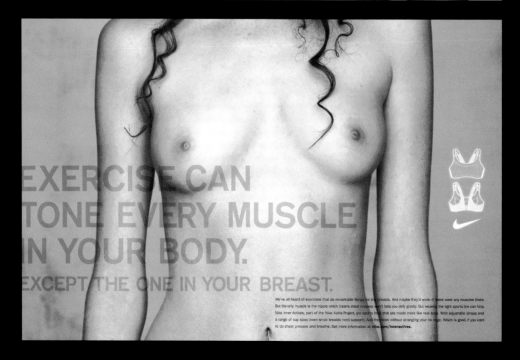

EXERCISE CAN TONE EVERY MUSCLE IN YOUR BODY. EXCEPT THE ONE IN YOUR BREAST.

We've all heard of exercises that do remarkable things for the breasts. And maybe they'd work—if there were any muscles there. But the only muscle is the nipple, which means chest presses won't help you defy gravity. But wearing the right sports bra can help. Nike Inner Actives, part of the Nike Alpha Project, are sports bras that are made more like real bras. With adjustable straps and a range of cup sizes (even small breasts need support). And they work without strangling your rib cage. Which is good, if you want to do chest presses and breathe. Get more information at **nike.com/inneractives.**

Agency: Richardson, Myers & Donofrio, Inc. Art Director: David Curtis Creative Director: Ken Majka Photographer: Jim Erikson Copywriter: Michael Neiderer Client: W.L. Gore Association

FRAUEN LIEBEN STILVOLLE MÄNNER.

MÄNNER LIEBEN GEPFLEGTE FRAUEN.

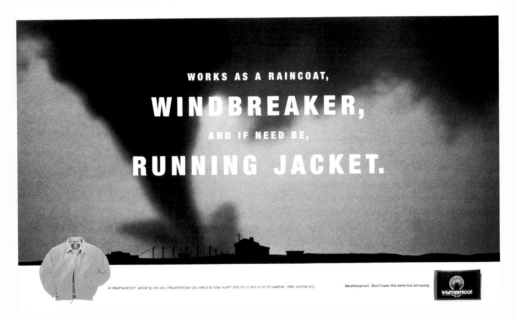

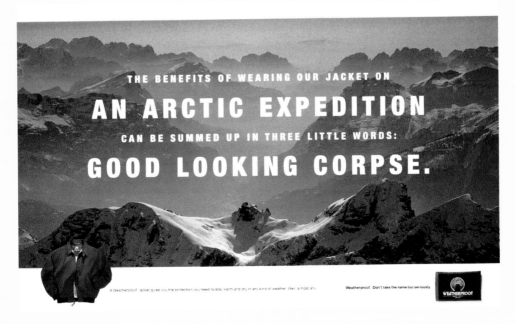

Agency: DeVito/Verdi Art Director: Mike Czako, Susanne Macarelli Creative Director: Sal DeVito Copywriter: Bob Fremgen, Joel Tractenberg Client: Weatherproof Jackets

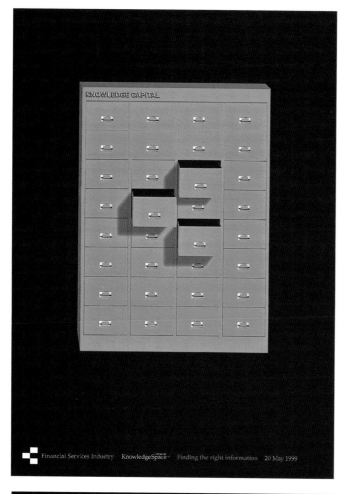

Financial Services Industry   KnowledgeSpace™   Finding the right information   20 May 1999

Financial Services Industry   KnowledgeSpace™   Discovering new directions   20 May 1999

Financial Services Industry   KnowledgeSpace™   Contributing to the bigger picture   20 May 1999

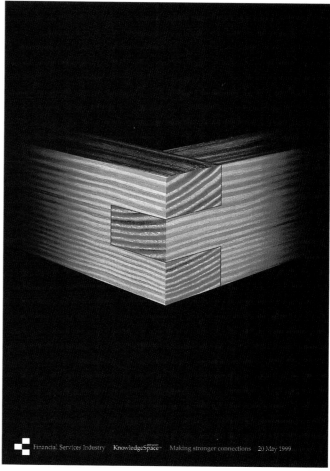

Financial Services Industry   KnowledgeSpace™   Making stronger connections   20 May 1999

Agency: Mytton Williams   Creative Director: Bob Mytton Designer: Stuart Youngs Photographer: John Matchett Client: Arthur Anderson

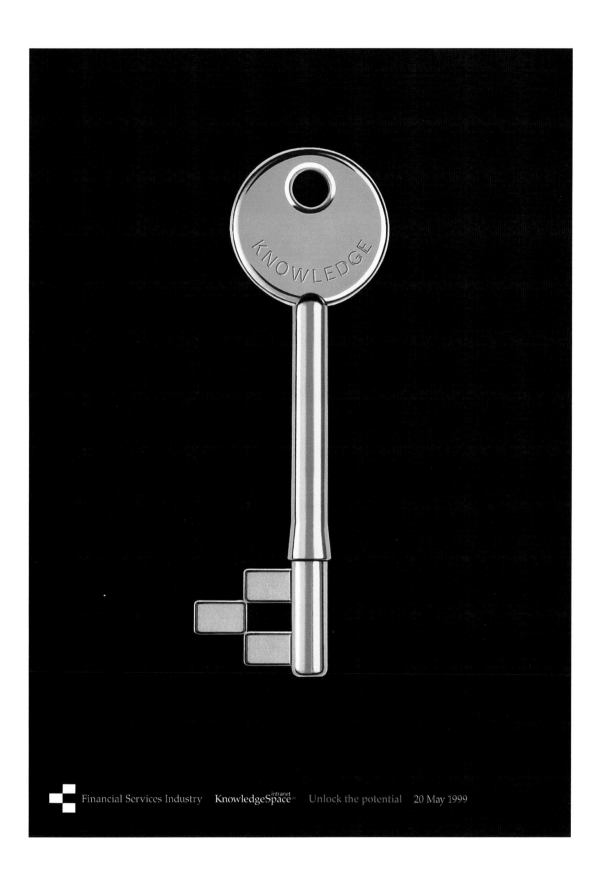

Financial Services Industry   KnowledgeSpace^{intranet}   Unlock the potential   20 May 1999

SOME LIKE IT COLD.™

The gum with pure & natural peppermint oil.

EVEREST
POWERFUL MINT GUM

©1999 Amurol Confections Co. www.everestgum.com

Agency: BBDO Chicago Art Director: Travis Britton Creative Director: Jim Hyman, Gail Pollack Photographer: Shawn Michienzi Copywriter: Jim Kelly Client: Amurol

It's 11pm. Do you know
where your JavaChip is?

PLEASE WAIT
TO BE SEATED

WHILE WE SCRAPE THE
FREEZER BURN OFF OUR
MASHED POTATOES

If you're not serving our mashed potatoes, you may be sending customers the wrong message.

Freezer burn won't be a problem when you are serving Northern Star fresh mashed potatoes. They're made from scratch, just like you'd prepare them, and their great taste tells customers you care about even the side dishes. Northern Star potatoes have a

40-day extended shelf life, which is the longest in the industry. Plain, seasoned, skin-on, or redskin, our mashed potatoes are a fresh solution that saves you time—and worry. Call Northern Star, the leader in refrigerated potatoes. 800-248-3447. www.michaelfoods.com

Thank You

It was a pleasure
serving you

bland reconstituted mashed potatoes

If you're not serving our mashed potatoes, you may be sending customers the wrong message.

Tasteless spuds won't be a problem when you are serving Northern Star fresh mashed potatoes. They're made from scratch, just like you'd prepare them, and their great taste tells customers you care about even the side dishes. Northern Star potatoes have a

40-day extended shelf life, which is the longest in the industry. Plain, seasoned, skin-on, or redskin, our mashed potatoes are a fresh solution that saves you time—and worry. Call Northern Star, the leader in refrigerated potatoes. 800-248-3447. www.michaelfoods.com

The mind-altering experience of VANILLA CASHEW CRUNCH

NO DIVING.

Dark Chocolate. Cool Mint. Low Fat. **Get the sensation.**

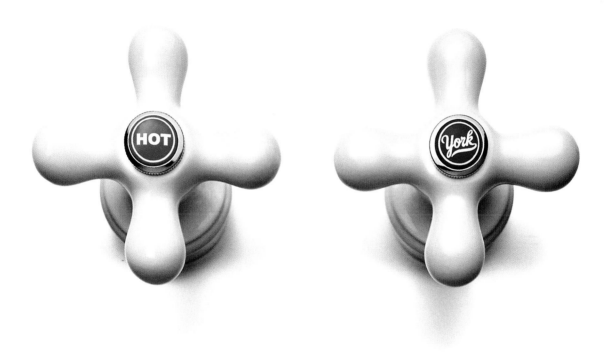

Dark Chocolate. Cool Mint. Low Fat. **Get the sensation.**

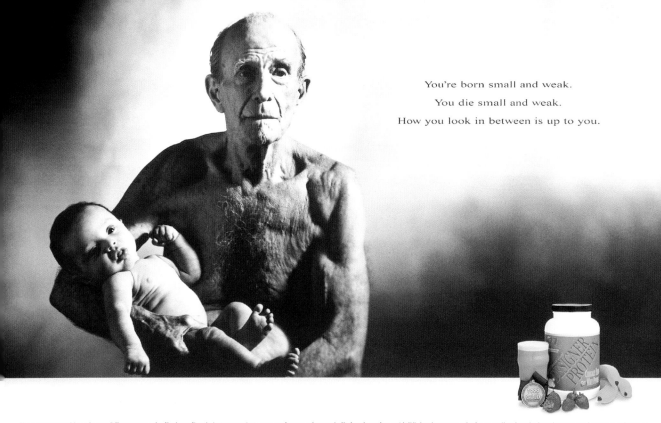

You're born small and weak.

You die small and weak.

How you look in between is up to you.

You want to grow big and strong? Get more protein. Designer Protein is proven to increase your lean muscle growth. End each workout with DP. Just because you're born small and weak, doesn't mean you have to stay that way.

Enjoy the natural honey taste.

Agency: BBDO Canada Art Director: Andrew Chang Creative Director: Michael McLaughlin, Jack Neary Photographer: Allan Davey Copywriter: Jill Atkinson Client: Kraft Canada

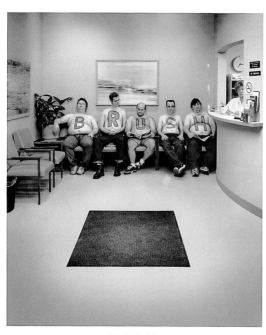

Note to dentists:
Be careful what you wish for.

The sonicare sonic toothbrush cleans with a combination of 31,000 brush strokes per minute and gentle sonic waves. sonicare also removes nearly twice as much plaque between teeth as a manual toothbrush. It's a one-two punch that gives your patients a clean feeling so unique, it'll turn just about anyone into a dental hygiene fanatic. In fact, we'll even guarantee your patients better checkups after just 90 days, or we'll give them their money back.

sonicare
It's not just a better toothbrush.
It's a better checkup.

Has a patient of yours ever
gotten this excited about dental hygiene?

The sonicare sonic toothbrush cleans with a combination of 31,000 brush strokes per minute and gentle sonic waves. sonicare also removes nearly twice as much plaque between teeth as a manual toothbrush. It's a one-two punch that gives your patients a clean feeling so unique, it'll turn just about anyone into a dental hygiene fanatic. In fact, we'll even guarantee your patients better checkups after just 90 days, or we'll give them their money back.

sonicare
It's not just a better toothbrush.
It's a better checkup.

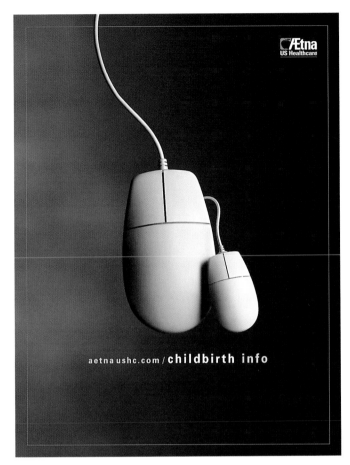

aetna ushc.com / **childbirth info**

aetna ushc.com / **better sleep tips**

aetna ushc.com / **vision care**

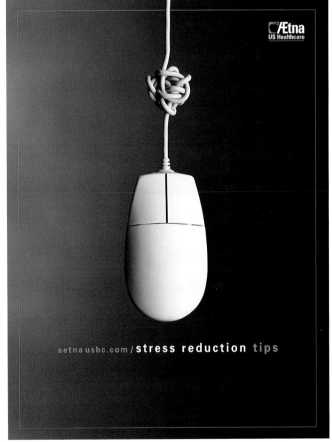

aetna ushc.com / **stress reduction tips**

Agency: McKinney & Silver Art Director: Mark Oakley Creative Director: David Baldwin Copywriter: Ken Marcus Client: Aetna US Healthcare

How do you plan on paying for home renovations?

If you build it, the bills will come. That's why at Conseco, we offer home equity loans as well as a wide range of other lending options to help you make your house your home. For more information, call toll-free 1-877-CONSECO, or visit our Web site at www.conseco.com.

INSURANCE INVESTMENTS LENDING

CONSECO.
Step up.®

How do you plan on funding your retirement?

They're called the golden years. But without smart financial planning they can feel more like nickel or copper. At Conseco, we offer a wide variety of annuities and mutual funds that can help you keep your head above water. For more information, call toll-free 1-877-CONSECO, or visit our Web site at www.conseco.com

INSURANCE INVESTMENTS LENDING

CONSECO.
Step up.®

How do you plan on paying unexpected medical bills?

Health care costs have reached an all-time high. But that doesn't mean you have to sink to an all-time low. At Conseco, we offer a wide range of supplemental health policies that can help when you need it most. For more information, call toll-free 1-877-CONSECO, or visit our Web site at www.conseco.com.

INSURANCE INVESTMENTS LENDING

CONSECO.
Step up.®

Agency: Fallon McElligott Art Director: Kevin Amter, Ellen Steinberg Photographer: Craig Cutler Client: Conseco

How do you plan on supporting your family after you're gone?

You worry about your family all your life. You shouldn't have to worry about them after it. Our companies offer a wide range of life insurance products that help provide for your family when you no longer can. So when your time comes, you can join the angels. Not the work force. *For more information, call toll-free 1-877-CONSECO, or visit our Web site at www.conseco.com.*

INSURANCE INVESTMENTS LENDING

CONSECO.
Step up."

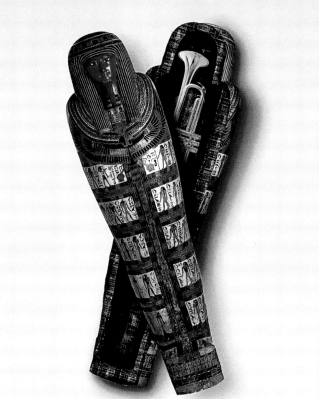

Agency: Ogilvy & Mather Art Director: Alfredo Rossi Creative Director: Bruce Lee Illustrator: Brooklyn Museum of Art, Magic Graphics Copywriter: Mark Drossman Client: Brooklyn Museum of Art

THE MUSEUM *for* TEXTILES GALA EVENT
Preparations are under way.

THE CURATORS DINNER / THURSDAY, OCTOBER 29TH 1998 / 8:00 PM / THE METROPOLITAN HOTEL / FOR TICKETS & INFORMATION, CALL 416.599.5321

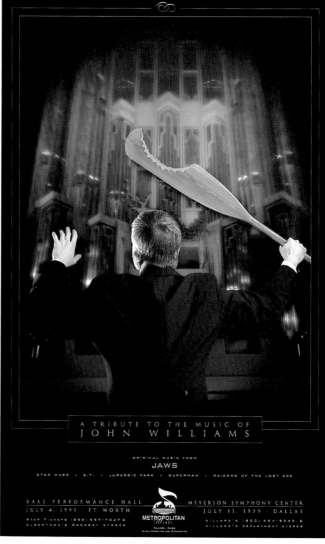

Agency: GSD&M Art Director: Matt Davis Photographer: Andrew Yates Copywriter: Kent Portman Client: Metropolitan Winds

ROCKABILLY HALL OF FAME   www.rockabillyhall.com

Agency: Hoffman York Pacific Art Director: Tim Mikus Creative Director: Tom Jordan Photographer: Peter Carter Copywriter: Nick Pipitone Client: Rockabilly Hall of Fame

HP Large Format Media benefit #32:

BRIGHTER IMAGES

When you need a sign that's as bright as your ideas, try HP Large Format media. These rigorously tested printing materials give you crisp colors and sharper images. Every time. For extra durability, try HP Colorfast Adhesive Vinyl. It makes your photos pop, sticks wherever you need it and lasts longer than a disco re-mix. HP printing material is engineered for HP Designjet printers and Ink Systems for a total printing solution. Improve your image. Ask for HP media. For a free sample roll of HP Paper-Based Semi-Gloss visit www.hpdesignjet-media.com.

HP Large Format Media benefit #27:

CONSISTENCY

What you print on is just as important as the printer itself. Only HP Large Format Media has the patented chemistry and extensive testing to give you superior color, clarity and consistency from print to print. And a wide variety of materials means it's perfect for nearly any job you can dream up. HP printing material is engineered for HP Designjet printers and Ink Systems for a total printing solution. Which means you spend less time printing and more time creating. Improve your image. Ask for HP. For more information visit www.hp.com/go/designjet.

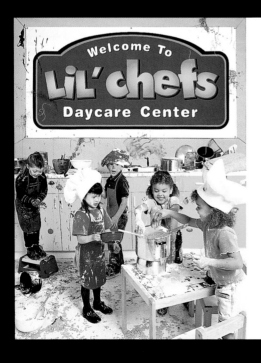

HP Large Format Media benefit #17:

DURABILITY

HP Banners with Tyvek® are a durable media for any application, indoors or out. When used with HP DesignJet CP Ink Systems UV, your signs are waterfast and fade resistant for up to three months without lamination. HP Banners with Tyvek give you superior color, consistency and durability from print to print. Improve your image. Ask for HP media. For a free sample roll of HP Paper-Based Semi-Gloss visit www.hpdesignjet-media.com.

Thompson Art Director: Rob Petrie Creative Director: Craig Evans Photographer: Chris Wimpey Copywriter: Craig Evans Clie

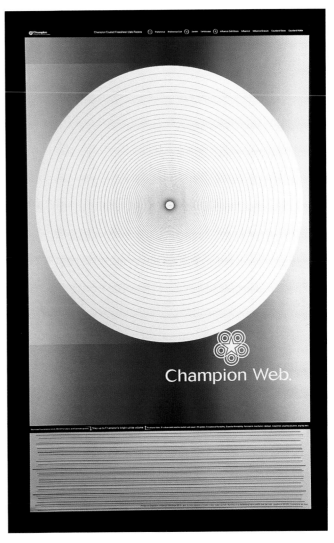

Agency: Jager Di Paola Kemp Art Director: David Covell Creative Director: Michael Jager Designer: David Covell Photographer: Wolfgang Ludes Copywriter: Laurel Saville Client: Champion Paper

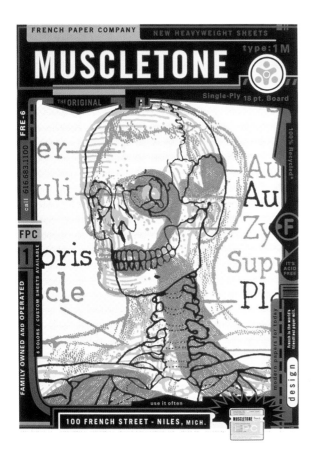

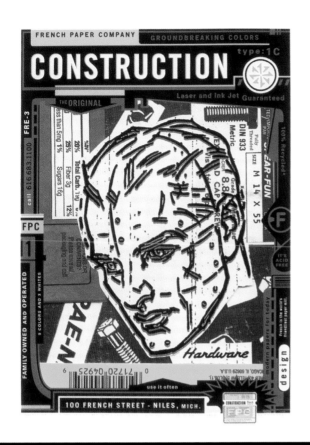

When you just must have pain relief in 15 minutes.

BRUFEN 600

BRUFEN 600

Fast relief from back pain.

When you just must have pain relief in 15 minutes.

BRUFEN 600

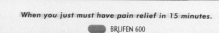

When you just must have pain relief in 15 minutes.

BRUFEN 600

Agency: SSC&B Lintas Art Director: Shantanu Gholkar Creative Director: Amar K. Deb, Shekhar Vaidya Copywriter: Amar K. Deb Client: Knoll Pharmaceuticals

Brian McConnell lives in the heart of maple syrup country up in Williston, Vermont. Home of more maple trees than just about anywhere.

On cold days when the sap's running slowly, you can find Brian playing guitar at one of the local breakfast places. And well, it just makes sense that Brian plays a Taylor made with maple sides and back.

He has a special appreciation for the maple tree. As do most people in Williston, especially the ones who've heard him play. In Brian's own words, "Syrup's not the sweetest thing to come out of a maple tree after all." Amen and pass the waffles.

65

Separated By Birth

16

Ron Arlin had to sell his first Taylor when his son was born. And he had to sell his second Taylor when his daughter was born. Then he had to sell his third Taylor when his other son was born. So now he has three kids. And no Taylors.

The good news is, in another fifteen years or so, those kids will move out and Ron can buy as many Taylors as he wants.

If there's one thing kids will teach you, it's patience.

164

Agency: Vitro Robertson Art Director: John Bade Creative Director: John Robertson, John Vitro Illustrators: *(top)* Zohar Lazar, *(bottom)* Mark Matcho, *(opposite, top)* Jonathan Carlson, *(opposite, bottom)* Ross MacDonald Copywriter: Brian Gold Client: Taylor Guitars Taylor Guitars

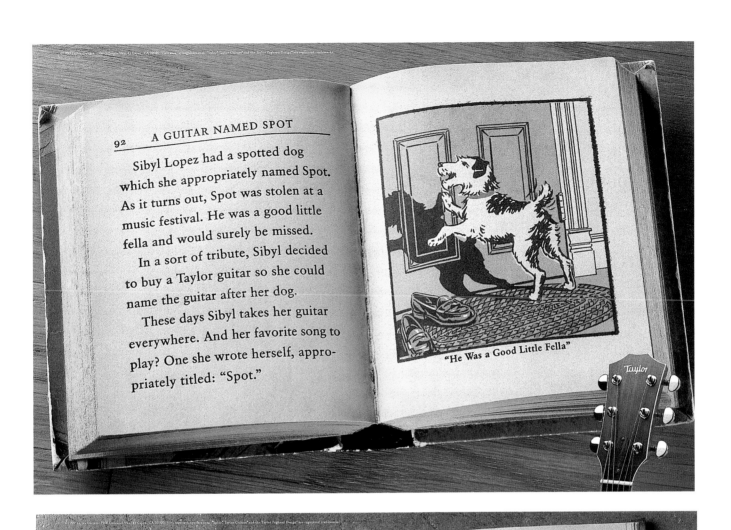

92   A GUITAR NAMED SPOT

Sibyl Lopez had a spotted dog which she appropriately named Spot. As it turns out, Spot was stolen at a music festival. He was a good little fella and would surely be missed.

In a sort of tribute, Sibyl decided to buy a Taylor guitar so she could name the guitar after her dog.

These days Sibyl takes her guitar everywhere. And her favorite song to play? One she wrote herself, appropriately titled: "Spot."

"He Was a Good Little Fella"

FROM STOCKHOLM TO STATEN ISLAND.
ONE MAN'S WANDERLUST IN THE KEY OF C.

People will often visit several stores in search of the perfect guitar. "Try two continents," says Torbjörn. He went off in search of a Taylor in Sweden but couldn't find one. So rather than give up, he kept going. Denmark, Germany, Holland. "What the heck. I'll just keep going," he said.

In London he bought a one-way ticket to New York. Where he hopped a ferry to Staten Island and visited a large music store. Not done yet, he continued on until he finally played a Taylor in Raleigh, North Carolina.

But wouldn't you know it, he ran out of money

and had to head back to Sweden—without the Taylor. As it turns out, three years later, Torbjörn finally got his Taylor. Most men would've given up. But then, Torbjörn has that Viking blood in him. And those Vikings sure do love an adventure.

34

35

Agency: Carmichael Lynch Art Director: Jeff Terwilliger Creative Director: Jud Smith Designer: Jeff Terwilliger Photographer: Ripsaw Copywriter: Steve Casey Client: Trex

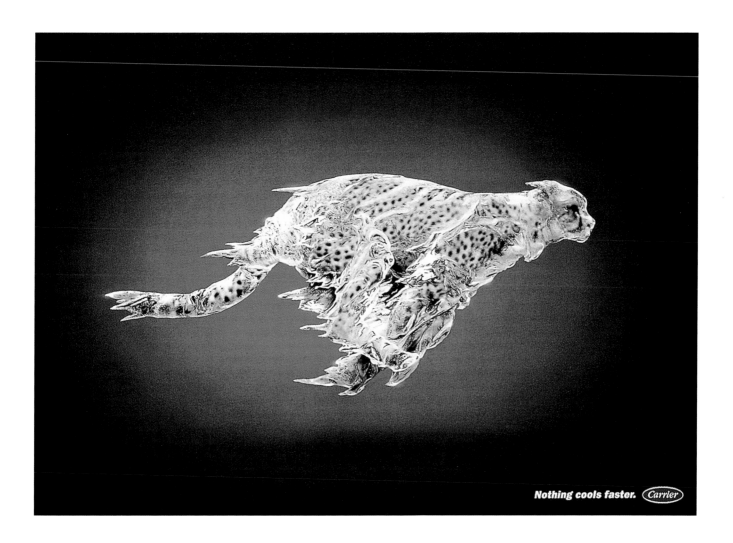

Agency: Ogilvy & Mather, Singapore Creative Director: Eric Yeo Photographer: Alex Kai Keong Illustrator: Lim Soon Huat Client: Carrier

True to the original.

invent

True to the original.

invent

True to the original.

invent

True to the original.

Life's vibrant color.

Subtle nuances of light and shadow.

Printouts that are most like your original photos.

The new hp DeskJet 970C.

Invent, create and inspire for just $399*

hp.com/go/original.

True to the original.

Discover life's vibrant colors.

Capture delicate detail and rich shadow.

Printouts that are most like your original photos.

The new hp DeskJet 970C.

Invent, create and inspire for just $399*

hp.com/go/original.

True to the original.

Realism that would impress a sand crab. Stunning detail.

Printouts that are most like your original photos,

without sacrificing razor-sharp text and graphics.

The new hp DeskJet 970C with up to 10 ppm color.

Invent, create and inspire for just $299*

Achieve superior results with hp supplies.

For more information, visit hp.com/go/original.

SOME PEOPLE AREN'T CUT OUT FOR WALLPAPER.

MAU

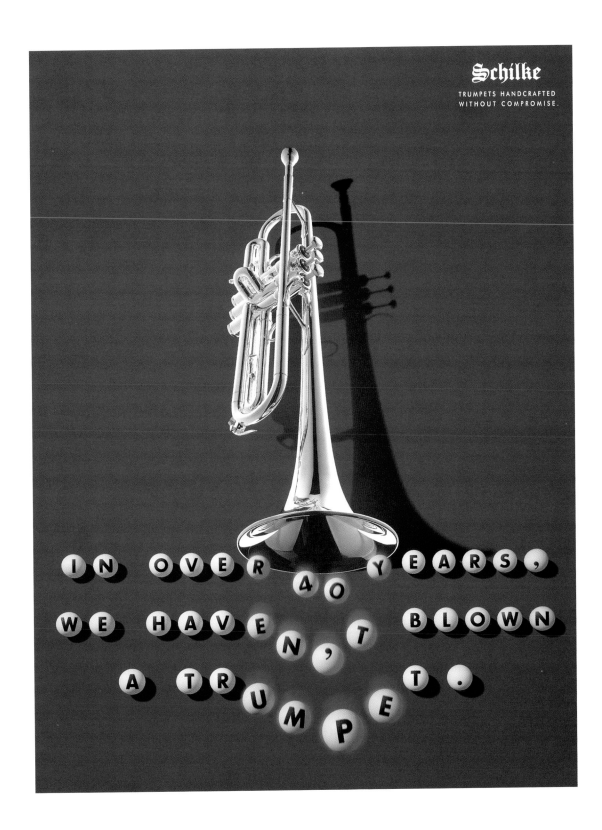

Agency: Hoffman York Art Director: Ken Butts Creative Director: Tom Jordan Photographer: Peter Carter Copywriter: Tom Jordan Client: Schilke Trumpets

The more stuff you have, the more stuff you have to fix. But the revolutionary new Wave™ can handle it all. And still fit in your pocket. Built with Tim Leatherman's obsessive attention to detail right here in Portland, Oregon.

■ = PERFECT USE FOR A LEATHERMAN • ONE TOOL. A COUPLE THOUSAND USES.® LEATHERMAN

It takes a lot of stuff to get away from it all. Tame the wilds and your campsite with the pocket-sized Leatherman. Crafted from stainless steel to Tim Leatherman's incredibly picky quality standards. We sweat the details so you can enjoy more important things. Like carving the perfect marshmallow stick.

▲ = PERFECT USE FOR A LEATHERMAN • ONE TOOL. A COUPLE THOUSAND USES.® LEATHERMAN

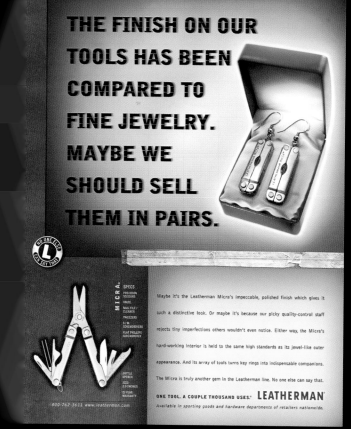

THE FINISH ON OUR TOOLS HAS BEEN COMPARED TO FINE JEWELRY. MAYBE WE SHOULD SELL THEM IN PAIRS.

Maybe it's the Leatherman Micra's impeccable, polished finish which gives it such a distinctive look. Or maybe it's because our picky quality-control staff rejects tiny imperfections others wouldn't even notice. Either way, the Micra's hard-working interior is held to the same high standards as its jewel-like outer appearance. And its array of tools turns key rings into indispensable companions. The Micra is truly another gem in the Leatherman line. No one else can say that.

ONE TOOL. A COUPLE THOUSAND USES. LEATHERMAN

Available in sporting goods and hardware departments of retailers nationwide.

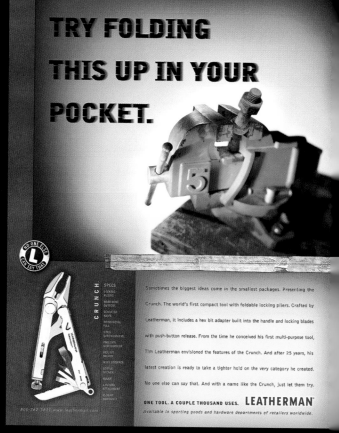

TRY FOLDING THIS UP IN YOUR POCKET.

Sometimes the biggest ideas come in the smallest packages. Presenting the Crunch. The world's first compact tool with foldable locking pliers. Crafted by Leatherman, it includes a hex bit adapter built into the handle and locking blades with push-button release. From the time he conceived his first multi-purpose tool, Tim Leatherman envisioned the features of the Crunch. And after 25 years, his latest creation is ready to take a tighter hold on the very category he created. No one else can say that. And with a name like the Crunch, just let them try.

ONE TOOL. A COUPLE THOUSAND USES. LEATHERMAN

Available in sporting goods and hardware departments of retailers worldwide.

THERE ARE STILL THINGS A
MACHINE CAN'T DO. THANK GOD.

Crescent® U.S.A.

919-781-7200 or www.coopertools.com COOPER Tools

DOESN'T FIT UNCALLUSED HANDS.

Crescent® U.S.A.

919-781-7200 or www.coopertools.com COOPER Tools

QUIKRETE CRACK SEAL

Agency: Fitzgerald & Co. Creative Director: James Paddock Art Director: Rob Kottkamp Designer: Rob Kottkamp Copywriter: Rob Kottkamp Client: Quikrete

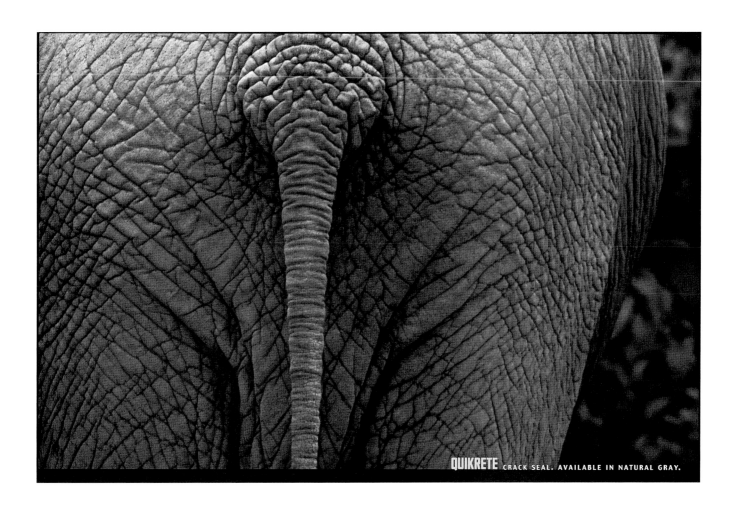

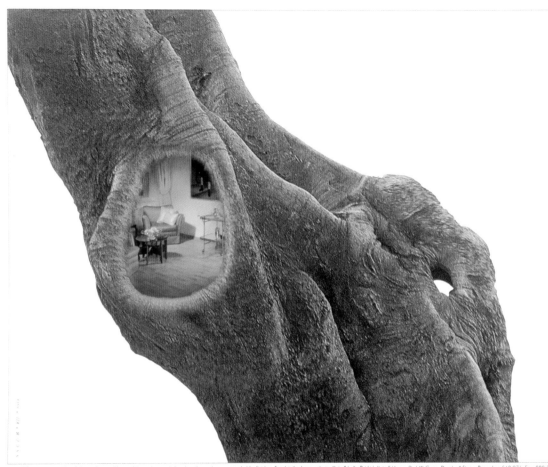

KAINDL
WOODEN FLOORING

Kaindl floors are available in light, medium and heavy duty, in cherry, ash, beech, oak, maple, spruce and alder finishes. For details please write to: Kaindl India Pvt Ltd. Kaindl House, 2nd 'A' Cross, Domlur II Stage, Bangalore 560 071. Fax: 080 5272731. e mail: kaindl@satyam.net

Agency: LKM Art Director: Doug Pedersen Creative Director: Jim Mountjoy Photographer: Mark Laita Copywriter: Curtis Smith Client: Mannington Floors

HOW ROMANTIC CAN A * 60 * WATT DINNER BE?

p i n e ḥ u r s t ◊ c a n d l e s

Durham, N.C.   919·489·1175

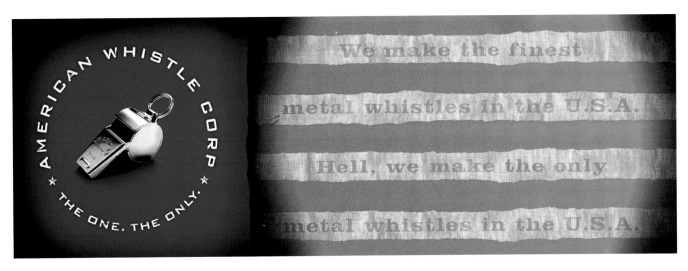

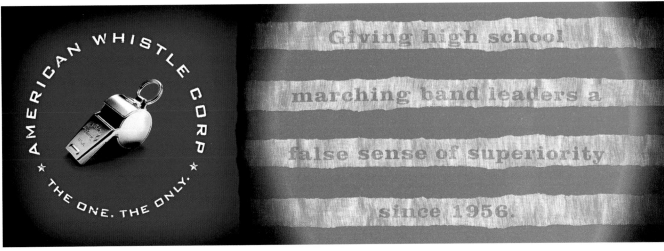

Agency: Buk/McDonald Art Director: Brent Goral Creative Director: Gary Mueller Photographer: Nancy Yuenkel Copywriter: Jeff Erickson Client: American Whistle

WER RETTET JETZT DEIN LEBEN?

FOCUS KONTAKTLINSEN.

Informieren, Probe tragen, Jo-Jo mitnehmen: Einfach 0800 - 83 84 85 anrufen.

Focus-Kontaktlinsen im 1-Monats-Austauschsystem machen das Leben leichter.
Deshalb: Jetzt beim Focus-Specialist informieren und Probe tragen. Ein Heavy-Jo-Jo gibt's zum Dank
auf jeden Fall. Übrigens: Focus sind auch bei Hornhautverkrümmung die richtige Wahl.

www.cibavision.com

Agency: Das Labor Art Director: Markus Weissenhorn Photographer: Sascha Kletzsch Copywriter: Michael Simpezl Client: Cibavision Switzerland

WER RETTET JETZT DEIN LEBEN?

FOCUS KONTAKTLINSEN.

Informieren, Probe tragen, Jo-Jo mitnehmen: Einfach 0800-83 84 85 anrufen.

Focus-Kontaktlinsen im 1-Monats-Austauschsystem machen das Leben leichter.
Deshalb: Jetzt beim Focus-Specialist informieren und Probe tragen. Ein Heavy-Jo-Jo gibt's zum Dank
auf jeden Fall. Übrigens: Focus sind auch bei Hornhautverkrümmung die richtige Wahl.

www.cibavision.com

WER RETTET JETZT DEIN LEBEN?

FOCUS KONTAKTLINSEN.

Informieren, Probe tragen, Jo-Jo mitnehmen: Einfach 0800-83 84 85 anrufen.

Focus-Kontaktlinsen im 1-Monats-Austauschsystem machen das Leben leichter.
Deshalb: Jetzt beim Focus-Specialist informieren und Probe tragen. Ein Heavy-Jo-Jo gibt's zum Dank
auf jeden Fall. Übrigens: Focus sind auch bei Hornhautverkrümmung die richtige Wahl.

www.cibavision.com

(top) Agency: Das Labor Art Director: Markus Weissenhorn Photographer: Sascha Kletzsch Copywriter: Michael Simpezl Client: Cibavision Switzerland
(bottom) Agency: Das Labor Art Director: Markus Weissenhorn Photographer: Ralf Kiefner Copywriter: Michael Simpezl Client: Cibavision Switzerland

(619) 350-8821

Agency: Matthews/Mark Art Director: Flint Cohen Creative Director: Michael Mark Photographer: Frank Short Copywriter: Michael Mark Client: Pacific Termite

sexual therapy • dr. víctor lleras • psychologist • 751-1110

Agency: Concepto Uno Art Director: Francisco Fernandez, Victor Lleras Creative Director: Victor Lleras Designer: Francisco Fernandez, Victor Lleras Copywriter: Francisco Fernandez, Victor Lleras Client: Dr. Victor Lleras

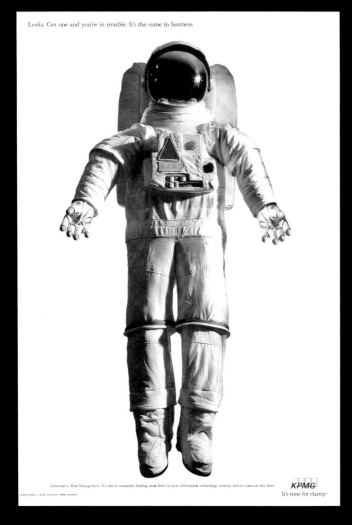

Leaks. Get one and you're in trouble. It's the same in business.

Information Risk Management. It's about constantly finding weak links in your information technology security, before someone else does.

KPMG
It's time for clarity.™

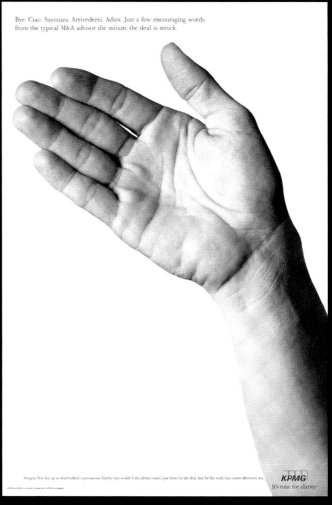

Bye. Ciao. Sayonara. Arrivederci. Adios. Just a few encouraging words from the typical M&A advisor the minute the deal is struck.

Mergers. Few live up to shareholders' expectations. Maybe they would if the advisor wasn't just there for the deal, but for the work that comes afterward, too.

KPMG
It's time for clarity.™

CAUTION: Mailing to people who have already said they don't want your offer can lead to shortness of breath when your boss inquires about the lower response rate and higher mailing cost. Get ChoiceMail. And get them off your list. The savings are guaranteed. 800-238-7658.

WARNING: Mailing to people who have already said they don't want your offer can lead to a dizzy feeling when you see the lower response rate and higher mailing cost. Get ChoiceMail. And get them off your list. The savings are guaranteed. 800-238-7658.

WARNING: Mailing to people who have already said they don't want your offer can lead to a queasy feeling in the pit of your stomach when the lower response rate and higher mailing cost are reported. Get ChoiceMail. And get them off your list. The savings are guaranteed. 800-238-7658.

With over ten years experience, no one is as efficient and skilled at removing dust and dirt quite like we are. Call 717-394-4006.

Eastern Air Inc.
AIR DUCT CLEANING

IT'S TAX SEASON AGAIN.

► ROBINSON & FAIREY, CPA'S, P.C. │ DUKE FOREST PLACE 3326 CHAPEL HILL BOULEVARD, SUITE B-130, DURHAM, NORTH CAROLINA 27707 │ **P**: (919) 489-5566 **F**: (919) 403-1480

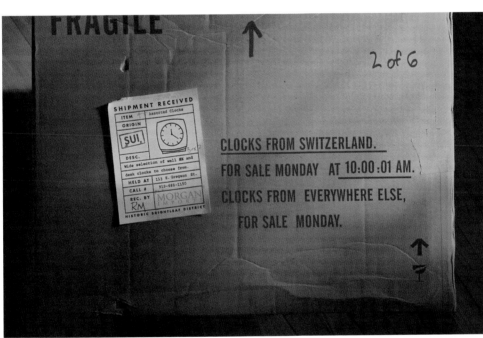

Agency: West & Vaughan Art Director: Rob Baird Creative Director: Robert Shaw West Designer: Rob Baird Photographer: Vic Cotto Illustrator: Mark Harkness Copywriter: Eran Thomson Client: Morgan Imports

How long has
it been since you
updated your
company's lighting?

Presenting innovative lighting services from Florida Power. With your permission, we'd like to shed a bit of light on improving productivity and lowering operating costs within your business. Once our account manager provides an unbiased and detailed analysis, he will make a recommendation on a variety of ways to improve lighting. Not to mention the most appropriate products to accomplish them with. In fact, if you like, we'll even arrange for the retrofit work to be completed. To be enlightened further on this subject, contact Jeff Merdich at 352-337-6903.

Florida Power

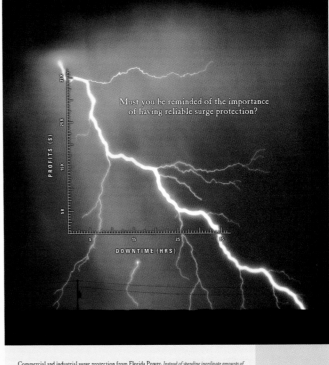

Must you be reminded of the importance
of having reliable surge protection?

PROFITS ($)

DOWNTIME (HRS)

Commercial and industrial surge protection from Florida Power. Instead of spending inordinate amounts of money repairing and replacing equipment damaged from surges, here's an idea. Eliminate the possibility altogether. Florida Power now offers surge protection that can be customized to your company's specific needs. Imagine, no more costly downtime. No more damaged equipment. No more premature graying. And when you put it in that context, the benefits are immeasurable. For more information, please contact Jeff Merdich at 352-337-6903.

Florida Power

"As an educator, I wanted our architect to see this school with a child's wonder. As a launching pad for imaginations. Where the environment itself is a teacher, and boredom has nowhere to hide." When you want an architect to build on your vision, call a member of The American Institute of Architects. AIA Architects, building on your vision.

AIA
THE AMERICAN INSTITUTE OF ARCHITECTS
Building on your vision.
aiaonline.com

Buildings that teach.

"I told my architect we wanted a place where ideas can't help but collide. A space that gives us an edge on the competition. Where the techi and the artist both feel at home. And work is what you escape to, not from." When you want an architect to build on your vision, call a member of The American Institute of Architects.

AIA
THE AMERICAN INSTITUTE OF ARCHITECTS
Building on your vision.
aiaonline.com

Buildings that engage.

(top left) Agency: Fahlgren/Tampa Art Director: Dan Nguyen Creative Director: Scott Sheinberg Photographer: Doug Johns Copywriter: James Rosene Client: Florida Power *(top right)* Agency: Fahlgren/Tampa Art Director: Dan Nguyen Creative Director: Scott Sheinberg Copywriter: James Rosene Client: Florida Power *(bottom)* Agency: Richardson, Myers & Donofrio, Inc. Art Director: David Curtis Creative Director: Ken Majka Photographer: Michael Furman Copywriter: Michael Neiderer Client: American Institute of Architects

Never underestimate the importance of foreseeing
a problem before it becomes one.

Presenting I-Scan™ infrared service from Florida Power. *One of the true measures of a successful business is the ability to foresee problems and correct them ahead of time. Our I-Scan infrared scanning service, for example, detects hot spots in your electrical system up to a year in advance. Using this state-of-the-art technology, our certified technicians can identify problems thus avoiding costly downtime, power outages, even potential fires. And in business, these are certainly the types of disasters to steer clear of. Contact Marsha Hoston at 1-888-340-2485.*

Florida Power

Agency: Fahlgren/Tampa Art Director: Dan Nguyen Creative Director: Scott Sheinberg Photographer: Doug Johns Illustrator: Liquid Pictures Copywriter: James Rosene Client: Florida Power

THE BOZELL SUMMER INTERNSHIP
(Seats available in every department.)

Agency: Bozell Group Art Director: David Steinke, Dustin Black Creative Director: David Moore Photographer: Bob Ervin Copywriter: Robin Leahy Client: Bozell Group

Agency: Heye & Partner GmbH Art Director: Oliver Oelkers Creative Director: Peter Hirrlinger, Ralph Taubenbeger Copywriter: Doris Haider Client: Tony Stone Bilderwelten

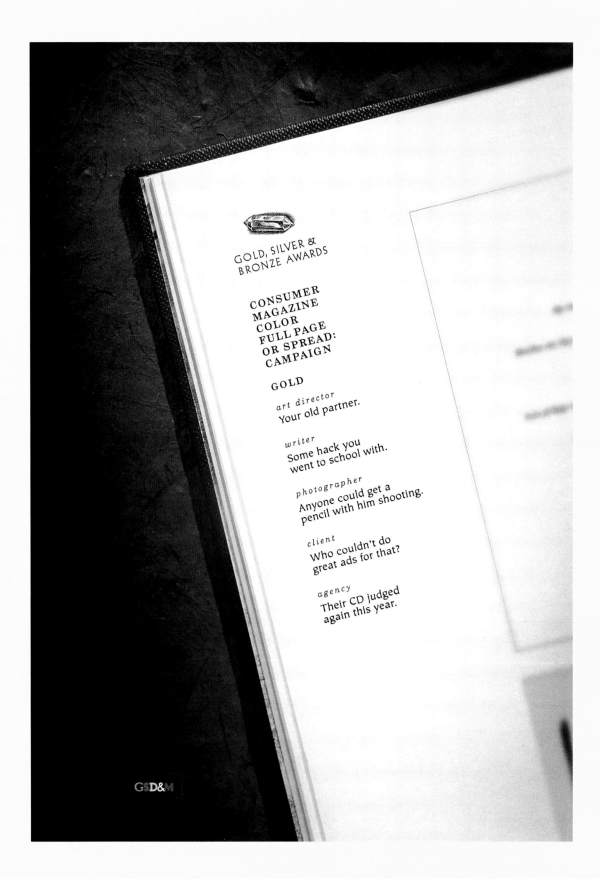

Agency: GSD&M Art Director: Lynn Sarnow Photographer: Dennis Fagan Copywriter: Bill Bayne Client: GSD&M

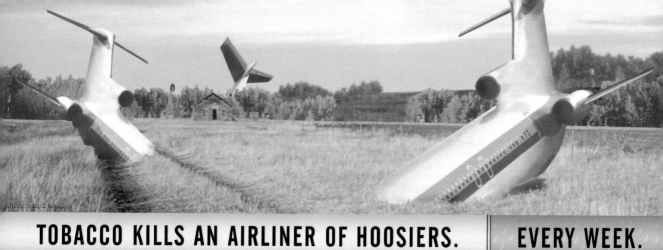

TOBACCO KILLS AN AIRLINER OF HOOSIERS. | **EVERY WEEK.**

TOBACCO KILLS A TITANIC OF HOOSIERS. | **EVERY 6 WEEKS.**

TOBACCO KILLS A BUSLOAD OF HOOSIERS. | **EVERY DAY.**

LIFE

Confidence is built upon the ability to overcome obstacles.

Special Olympics
NEBRASKA

Agency: Bailey Lauerman Art Director: Carter Weitz Creative Director: Carter Weitz Photographer: David Radler Copywriter: John Vogel Client: Special Olympics

Agency: Buk/McDonald Art Director: Chris Buhrman Creative Director: Gary Mueller Photographer: Brian Malloy Copywriter: Chris Buhrman Client: Wisconsin Donor Network

(top) Agency: Butler, Shine & Stern Art Director: Hilary Wolfe Creative Director: John Butler, Mike Shine Photographer: Brian Mahany Copywriter: Ryan Ebner Client: San Francisco Dept. of Public Health *(bottom)* Agency: GSD&M Art Director: Sean Keith Copywriter: Clint Carter Client: SADD Austin Chapter

Agency: Kohnke Hanneken Milwaukee Art Director: Peter Schaer Creative Director: Dave Hanneken, Rich Kohnke Photographer: Tim Waite Illustrator: Jim McDonald Copywriter: Rob Franks Client: Wisconsin Humane Society

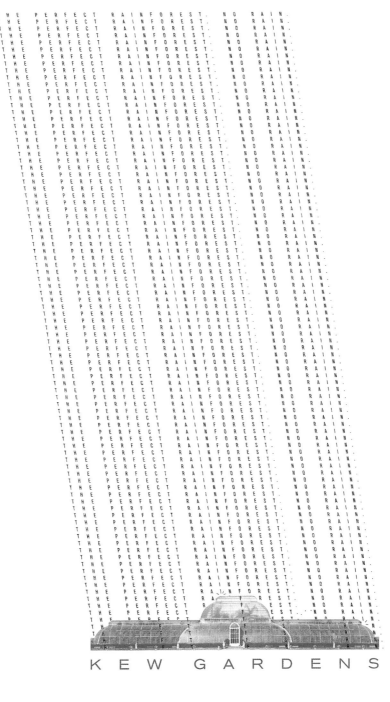

KEW GARDENS

Agency: SSC&B Lintas Art Director: Umesh Bhagat Creative Director:Vikram Gaikwad Client: Society for Alcohol Related Social Policy Initiative

HELP US PICK UP THE THINGS THAT DON'T BELONG IN NATURE.
BIG SWEEP 1999. SATURDAY, SEPTEMBER 18.

Work for litter-free waters across North Carolina. For clean-up locations,
call 1-800-27SWEEP, or visit www.landmark-project.com/bigsweep

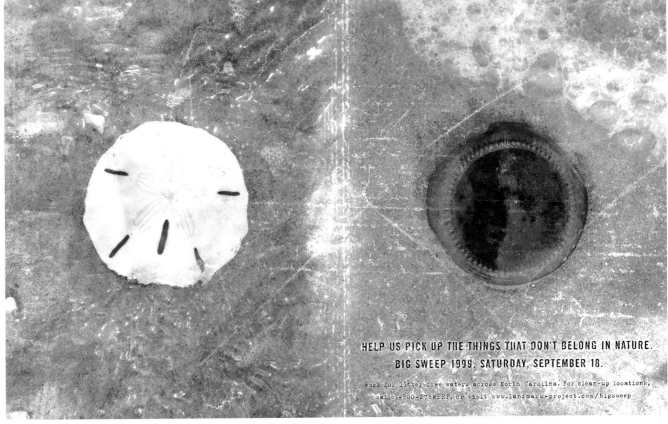

HELP US PICK UP THE THINGS THAT DON'T BELONG IN NATURE.
BIG SWEEP 1999. SATURDAY, SEPTEMBER 18.

Work for litter-free waters across North Carolina. For clean-up locations,
call 1-800-27SWEEP, or visit www.landmark-project.com/bigsweep

Agency: FGI, Inc. Art Director: David Roberts Creative Director: Denzil Strickland Designer: David Roberts Photographer: James Schwartz, Bus 9 Copywriter: Denzil Strickland
Client: North Carolina Big Sweep

Which man looks guilty? If you picked the man on the right, you're wrong.

your rights. Support the ACLU. www.aclu.org **american civil liberties union**

On February 4th, 1999, the NYPD gave Amadou Diallo the right to remain silent. And they did it without ever saying a word. Firing 41 bullets in 8 seconds, the police killed an unarmed, innocent man. Also wounded was the constitutional right of every American to due process of law. Help us defend your rights. Support the ACLU. www.aclu.org **american civil liberties union**

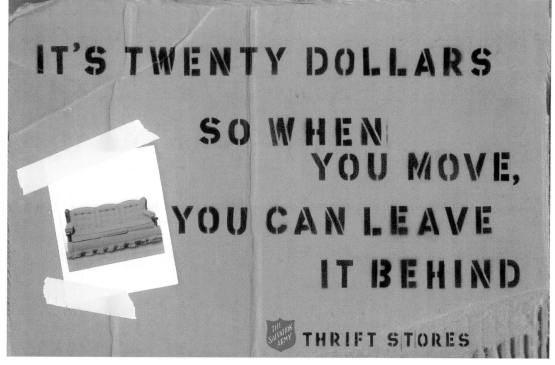

Agency: CCFC Advertising Art Director: Michelle Hoagland Creative Director: Mike Cheney, Ben Counts Designer: Michelle Hoagland Copywriter: Andy Tillman Client: Salvation Army

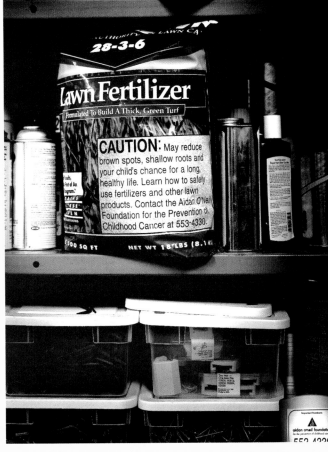

Agency: Bozell Group Art Director: Mitch Markussen, David Steinke, Ron Sack Photographer: Bob Ervin Copywriter: Robin Leahy Client: Aidan O'Neil Foundation

THE CONTENTS OF A HOT DOG MAY VARY.

BUT THE ONE THING THEY ALL HAVE IN COMMON IS A CASING, ALSO KNOWN AS THE SKIN OF THE HOT DOG. CASINGS CONSIST OF MANY THINGS, NATURAL AND ARTIFICIAL. ORIGINALLY, THEY WERE MADE FROM THE INTESTINES OF HOGS, SHEEP OR CATTLE. BUT IT'S WHAT YOU PUT INSIDE THE CASING THAT REALLY MAKES IT A HOT DOG. ACCORDING TO FRANK ASHBROOK, AUTHOR OF *BUTCHERING, PROCESSING AND PRESERVATION OF MEAT*, THE HOT DOG IS THE MOST POPULAR COOKED SAUSAGE IN THE WORLD. WIENERS (AS THEY ARE COMMONLY CALLED) ARE COOKED, SMOKED, THEN COOKED AGAIN BEFORE SERVING. THE WIENER THAT YOU AND I ARE MOST ACCUSTOMED TO USUALLY — AND I STRESS USUALLY — CONTAINS BEEF, PORK, WATER, SAGE, MACE OR NUTMEG, AND SALT AND PEPPER. THE CASINGS ARE STUFFED WITH THIS MIXTURE AND HUNG IN A SMOKEHOUSE FOR ABOUT TWO HOURS, OR UNTIL THEY TURN A RICH ORANGE COLOR. YUMMY. THEN THEY'RE BOILED UNTIL THEY FLOAT. WHERE DO THE PORK AND BEEF COME FROM? I'M GLAD YOU ASKED. ASHBROOK TELLS US THAT "IN LARGE PACKING HOUSES, MEAT BY-PRODUCTS LIKE HOT DOGS ARE MADE EXCLUSIVELY OF TRIMMINGS, SCRAPS, HARD-TO-SELL IRREGULAR CUTS OF MEAT AND OTHER PARTS OF THE CARCASS NOT INCLUDED IN THE STANDARD CUTS." IN SHORT, WHO KNOWS? BUT, GOSH DARNIT, THEY TASTE AWFUL GOOD. THE AUTHORS OF *THE PRINCIPLES OF MEAT SCIENCE* CONCUR WITH ASHBROOK ON THE VARIOUS INGREDIENTS FOUND IN SOME COOKED SAUSAGE. THESE INGREDIENTS, COMMONLY REFERRED TO AS "FILLER MEATS" MAY INCLUDE TRIPE, LIPS, STOMACHS, SKIN AND SNOUTS. HOWEVER, THERE IS GOOD NEWS. THE AMOUNT OF THESE FILLERS MUST BE LIMITED. WHY? BASICALLY, BECAUSE THESE PARTICULAR MEATS ARE SO RICH IN COLLAGEN THAT THEY DON'T BIND WELL WHEN LARGE AMOUNTS ARE PRESENT. TOO BAD, HUH? BUT FILLER MEATS AND MEAT BY-PRODUCTS DO HAVE SOME BENEFITS. SAUSAGES MADE WITH VARIETY MEATS ARE EQUAL — IF NOT SUPERIOR — TO SAUSAGES MADE WITH ONLY SKELETAL MEAT. EVEN SO, MEAT INSPECTION REGULATIONS STILL REQUIRE COOKED SAUSAGES TO LIST ALL INGREDIENTS ON A PACKAGING LABEL. SUCH A LABEL ISN'T USUALLY REQUIRED TO SPECIFICALLY MENTION PORK JOWLS, BREASTS, EARS, CHEEK MEAT, LUNGS, HEARTS, SPLEENS, BRAINS, OR NON-LACTATING UDDERS. MOST PROCESSORS ARE ALLOWED TO GET AWAY WITH SIMPLY PRINTING "FRANKFURTERS MADE WITH VARIETY MEATS" IN A TINY TYPESIZE THAT THE MAJORITY OF SHOPPERS WILL NEVER SEE. DON'T WORRY — IF YOU MAKE HOMEMADE HOT DOGS, YOU'LL KNOW EXACTLY WHAT'S IN THEM. IF YOU'RE SURE THAT'S WHAT YOU WANT. LUE AND ED PARK, CO-AUTHORS OF *THE SMOKED FOODS COOKBOOK*, PROVIDE THE ULTIMATE HOW-TO ON HOME SAUSAGE MAKING. STEP ONE? ONCE YOU HAVE YOUR MEAT (BY-PRODUCT OR OTHERWISE), CUT IT INTO SMALL CHUNKS OR COOKING PORTIONS SO THAT IT GOES THROUGH THE GRINDER EASILY. THEY ALSO TELL YOU TO CUT AWAY ANY CARTILE, TENDON, BLOOD CLOTS, BLOODSHOT MEAT AND EXCESS FAT BEFORE SUBJECTING THE MEAT TO THE GRINDER. AND MAKE SURE YOUR GRINDER HAS SHARP BLADES. DULL BLADES WILL MASH MEAT SO THAT IT LOSES ITS NATURAL JUICES AND TEXTURE. NOW COMES THE FUN PART — DECIDING WHAT TYPE OF SAUSAGE YOU'LL MAKE. WHAT YOU PUT IN YOUR SAUSAGE IS ENTIRELY UP TO YOU AND YOUR INDIVIDUAL TASTES. DID YOU KNOW THAT COUNTRIES DEVELOP SAUSAGE RECIPES BASED ON THE INGREDIENTS FOUND IN THEIR PARTICULAR REGIONS? LUE AND ED TELL US THAT PEOPLE IN SCOTLAND USE OATMEAL IN THEIR SAUSAGES. RECIPES FROM LUXEMBOURG INCLUDE CABBAGE. NATIVE AMERICANS MAKE A TYPE OF SAUSAGE OUT OF VENISON, BUFFALO JERKY, FAT AND DRIED BERRIES. ITALIANS PREPARE SAUSAGE WITH WINE, AND THE GERMANS, PERHAPS BEST KNOWN FOR THEIR BRATWURST AND SAUERKRAUT, ADD FLAVOR TO THEIR SAUSAGE WITH BEER. AS LONG AS YOU'RE USING QUALITY INGREDIENTS, THERE'S NO LIMIT TO THE TYPES OF SAUSAGE YOU CAN CREATE. ALMOST ANYTHING — FROM CHICKEN, TURKEY, DUCK, GOOSE, LOBSTER, SCALLOPS AND SHRIMP TO MANY SALTWATER FISH — CAN BE USED TO MAKE DELICIOUS AND MEMORABLE SAUSAGES. IT DOESN'T REALLY MATTER WHAT YOU CHOOSE AS LONG AS IT'S FLOP-ON-THE-PLATE FRESH. WHY CHECK THE EXPIRATION DATE? ACCORDING TO CHARLES G. REAVIS, AUTHOR OF *HOME SAUSAGE MAKING*, WHEN YOU GRIND MEAT, THE ACTUAL PROCESS CREATES GREATER SURFACE AREA IN RELATION TO THE WEIGHT OF THE MEAT. MORE SURFACE AREA MEANS A LARGER BREEDING GROUND FOR CERTAIN TYPES OF BACTERIA. OF COURSE, ALL MEAT CONTAINS SOME BACTERIA. THE GOAL IN MAKING YOUR OWN SAUSAGE IS PREVENTING THAT BACTERIA FROM REPRODUCING AND POSSIBLY TAINTING YOUR CREATION. IN SHORT, THE FRESHER THE BETTER. WHILE WE'RE ON THE SUBJECT, YOU MIGHT WONDER HOW LONG SAUSAGE HAS BEEN AROUND. GREEK SAUSAGE, OR *ORYA*, WAS WRITTEN ABOUT IN THE *ODYSSEY* — AN ANCIENT EPIC WRITTEN AROUND 700 B.C. THE ACTUAL TERM *SAUSAGE* IS DERIVED FROM THE LATIN WORD *SALSUS*, WHICH MEANS "SALTED" EARLY MAN USED SALT TO FLAVOR AND PRESERVE FRESH MEAT. THAT'S HOW IT ALL STARTED. SINCE THEN, THE WORLD'S PASSION FOR SAUSAGE HAS CONTINUED TO GROW. IN *THE BOOK OF THE PIG*, JACK DENTON SCOTT TELLS US THAT 75 MILLION PIGS GO TO MARKET IN THE UNITED STATES ANNUALLY. ALMOST EVERY PART OF THE PIG IS USED. SOME SIXTY-FIVE PERCENT IS PROCESSED AS FOOD, WHILE THE REST GOES TO MAKE MANY OF THE PRODUCTS WE USE EVERYDAY — FROM GLUE TO LIFE-SAVING MEDICINES. UNLIKE MANY HUMANS, ALL PIGS SEEM TO HAVE AN ORGAN DONOR CARD. THOUSANDS OF HUMANS ARE ALIVE TODAY BECAUSE THEY RECEIVE A HEART VALVE FROM A PIG. AND DOCTORS HAVE BEEN USING PIGSKIN FOR YEARS TO HELP SEVERELY BURNED HUMAN SKIN REGENERATE. BUT EVEN WITH THIS IMPRESSIVE LIST, MANY STILL BELIEVE THAT THE PIG'S MOST IMPORTANT CONTRIBUTION IS — YOU GUESSED IT — THE CHILI DOG. STILL HUNGRY FOR MORE INFORMATION? GO TO THE OMAHA PUBLIC LIBRARY. YOU'LL FIND EVERYTHING FROM HOT DOGS TO HERNIAS — IN RESOURCES LIKE NEWSPAPERS, MAGAZINES, BOOKS, AND THE INTERNET, OR OUR ONLINE COMPUTER LIBRARY CENTER THAT GIVES YOU ACCESS TO MORE THAN 30,000 LIBRARIES IN 63 DIFFERENT COUNTRIES. DID WE MENTION OUR TRAINED STAFF OF LIBRARIANS? OR OUR FAX SERVICES? AND DON'T FORGET THE MORE THAN 18,000 VIDEOS, CDS AND AUDIO TAPES YOU CAN CHECK OUT...

THE OMAHA PUBLIC LIBRARY.
EVERYTHING YOU WANTED TO KNOW. AND MORE.

Agency: Bozell Group Art Director: Mitch Markussen, David Steinke Copywriter: Robin Leahy, Jackie Ostrowich Client: Omaha Public Library

WHEN IT'S FOURTH AND GOAL
AND YOU'RE DOWN BY SIX
"UNNECESSARY ROUGHNESS"
IS A CONTRADICTION IN TERMS.

YOU MAY NOT GET IT.
BUT OUR 25 MILLION READERS DO.

Sports Illustrated

THERE'S A 95 MPH PROJECTILE
SCREAMING TOWARD HIS FACE.
AND THE ONLY THING HE'S AFRAID OF
IS THAT IT MIGHT NOT HIT HIM.

YOU MAY NOT GET IT.
BUT OUR 25 MILLION READERS DO.

Sports Illustrated

(top) Agency: Fallon McElligott Art Director: Steve Driggs Creative Director: David Lubars Designer: Jason Strong Photographer: Peter Diana, Pittsburgh Post Gazette
Copywriter: Greg Hahn Client: Sports Illustrated *(bottom)* Agency: Fallon McElligott Art Director: Steve Driggs Creative Director: David Lubars Designer: Jason
Strong Photographer: David Klutho Copywriter: Greg Hahn Client: Sports Illustrated

(top) Agency: Fallon McElligott Art Director: Steve Driggs Creative Director: David Lubars Designer: Jason Strong Photographer: John W. McDonough
Copywriter: Greg Hahn Client: Sports Illustrated (bottom) Agency: Fallon McElligott Art Director: Steve Driggs Creative Director: David Lubars Designer: Jason
Strong Photographer: George Tiedeman Copywriter: Greg Hahn Client: Sports Illustrated

TIME

We'll miss trying to keep

up with him.

The world's most interesting magazine.

TIME

There are two kinds of stories.

Those you want to see.

And those you must see.

The world's most interesting magazine.

TIME

Financial news, from the

budget deficit all the way up

to the Jagger settlement.

The world's most interesting magazine.

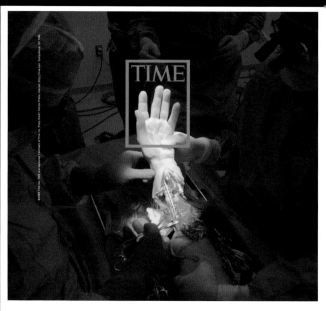

TIME

Some photos have their own special beauty.

Here, the first transplanted hand.

The world's most interesting magazine.

(top, left) Agency: Fallon McElligott Art Director: Bob Barrie Creative Director: David Lubars Designer: Bob Barrie Photographer: John W. McDonough
Copywriter: Dean Buckhorn Client: Time *(top, right)* Agency: Fallon McElligott Art Director: Bob Barrie Creative Director: David Lubars Designer: Bob Barrie
Photographer: Paul Lowe Copywriter: Dean Buckhorn Client: Time *(bottom, left)* Agency: Fallon McElligott Art Director: Bob Barrie Creative Director: David
Lubars Designer: Bob Barrie Photographer: Stephanee Cardinale Copywriter: Dean Buckhorn Client: Time *(bottom, right)* Agency: Fallon McElligott Art Director:
Bob Barrie Creative Director: David Lubars Designer: Bob Barrie Photographer: Patrick Pfister Copywriter: Dean Buckhorn Client: Time

A Story About a Couple of Cities

It was a cool time, it was a crummy time. It was the age of really smart people, it was the age of dummies. It was really going back and forth. Good, bad, good, bad, you get the idea.

What if writers didn't push themselves?

USA WEEKEND magazine's annual Student Fiction Contest encourages students to read the newspaper for ideas on themes, plots and character development. Then write a story based on what they've learned. It's part of an in-class curriculum designed to inspire young writers. So they, in turn, can inspire us. For information on this and many other USA WEEKEND Newspaper In Education opportunities (including NIE circulation grants), call Dave Barber, Vice President/Newspaper Relations, at 212.715.2131 or contact your local USA WEEKEND magazine representative.

Agency: Work Art Director: Mike Boulia, Creative Director: Cabell Harris, Copywriter: Anne Marie Floyd, Client: USA Weekend Magazine

Wirtschaft hat viele Seiten.

Süddeutsche Zeitung
Deutschlands große Tageszeitung

Wer sie liest, sieht mehr.

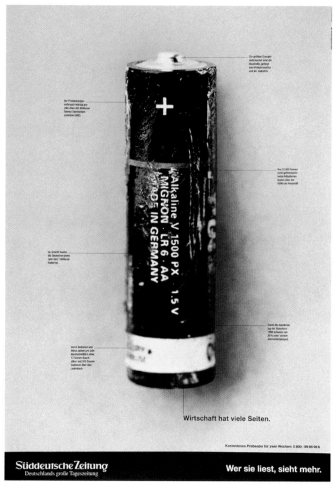

Wirtschaft hat viele Seiten.

Süddeutsche Zeitung
Deutschlands große Tageszeitung

Wer sie liest, sieht mehr.

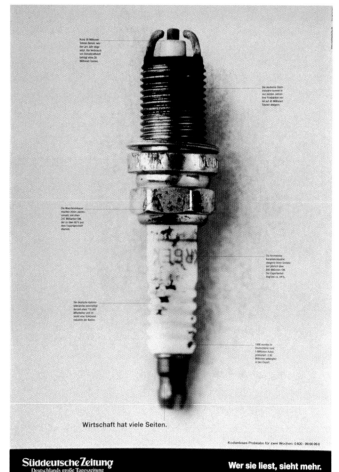

Wirtschaft hat viele Seiten.

Süddeutsche Zeitung
Deutschlands große Tageszeitung

Wer sie liest, sieht mehr.

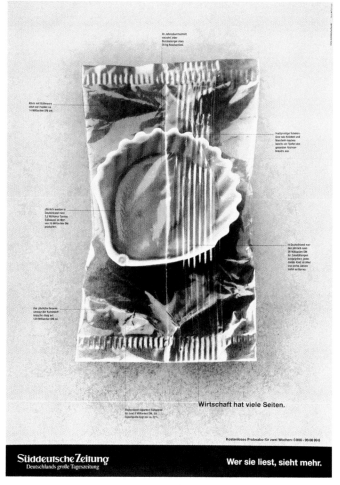

Wirtschaft hat viele Seiten.

Süddeutsche Zeitung
Deutschlands große Tageszeitung

Wer sie liest, sieht mehr.

Agency: Heye & Partner GmbH Art Director: Beate Gronemann Creative Director: Ralph Taubenberger, Peter Hirrlinger Designer: Monika Raber Photographer: Raoul Manuel Schnell Copywriter: Otward Buchner Client: Süddeutsche Zeitung

Agency: DeVito/Verdi Art Director: Eric Schutte, Lee Seidenberg Creative Director: Sal DeVito Copywriter: Eric Schutte Lee Seidenberg Client: People Profiles

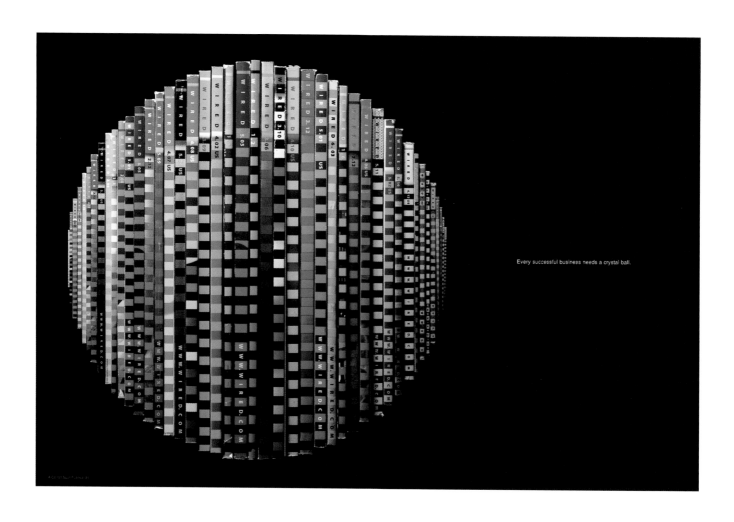

Every successful business needs a crystal ball.

Agency: Black Rocket Art Director: Bob Kerstetter, Steve Stone Creative Director: Bob Kerstetter, Steve Stone Photographer: Dan Escobar Copywriter: Bob Kerstetter Client: Wired

Agency: Mazzy-Noe Advertising, Chicago Art Director: Dolph Kawalec Creative Director: Dolph Kawalec, Dave Kwasnick Photographer: Chris Cassidy Copywriter: Dave Kwasnick
Client: Kafein Cafe and Espresso Bar

RENT A VIDEO

MAKE A VIDEO

Shuckers Oyster Bar. *For the ultimate shuck*®
919.556.7704 Wake Forest, NC

BONDING

BONDAGE

Shuckers Oyster Bar. *For the ultimate shuck*®
919.556.7704 Wake Forest, NC

CALL ME

CALL ME MOMMY

Shuckers Oyster Bar. *For the ultimate shuck*®
919.556.7704 Wake Forest, NC

TWIN BEDS

IN BED WITH TWINS

Shuckers Oyster Bar. *For the ultimate shuck*®
919.556.7704 Wake Forest, NC

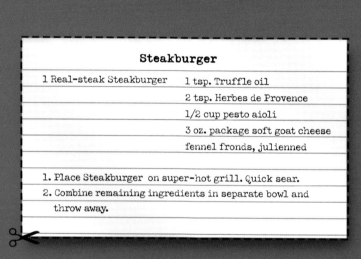

Steakburger

1 Real-steak Steakburger	1 tsp. Truffle oil
	2 tsp. Herbes de Provence
	1/2 cup pesto aioli
	3 oz. package soft goat cheese
	fennel fronds, julienned

1. Place Steakburger on super-hot grill. Quick sear.
2. Combine remaining ingredients in separate bowl and throw away.

We don't put a lot of fancy
ingredients in our Steakburgers.
Just cuts of real steak.
And since 1934, that's been
more than enough.

Open 24 hours.

More than 40 greater St. Louis locations.

Agency: Young & Laramore Art Director: Jeff Morris Creative Director: Charles Hopper Copywriter: David Nehamkin Client: Steak 'n Shake

Agency: Wonderstorm Design, LLC Art Director: Peter Groben Creative Director: Peter Groben Designer: Peter Groben Illustrator: Peter Groben Copywriter: Peter Groben Client: The Drafting Room

(recess)

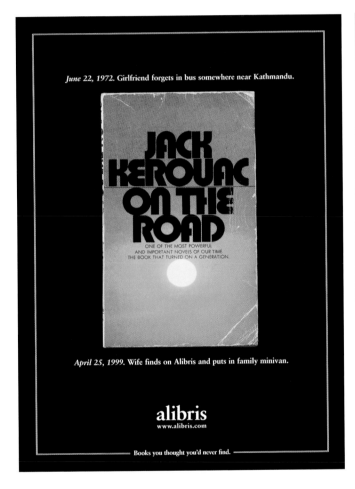

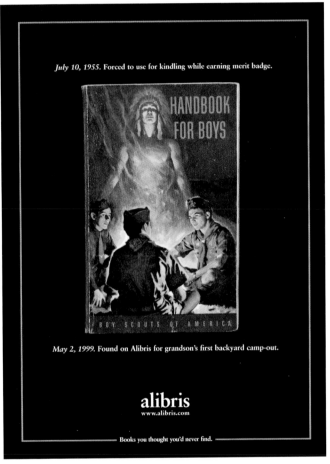

Agency: Saatchi & Saatchi Art Director: Kevin Samuels Creative Director: Curtis Melville, Steve Silver Copywriter: David Knox Client: alibris.com

Agency: Fallon McElligott Art Director: Scott O'Leary Creative Director: David Lubars Photographer: John Clang Copywriter: Michael Burdick Client: nordstromshoes.com

(top) Agency: Fallon McElligott Art Director: Scott O'Leary Creative Director: David Lubars Photographer: John Clang Copywriter: Michael Burdick Client: nordstromshoes.com *(bottom)* Agency: Fallon McElligott Art Director: Scott O'Leary Creative Director: David Lubars Photographer: Joe Paczkowski Copywriter: Michael Burdick Client: nordstromshoes.com

Agency: SMC Art Director: Shari Hindman Designer: Shari Hindman Photographer: David Harry Stewart Copywriter: Roy Davimes Client: Jersey Gardens

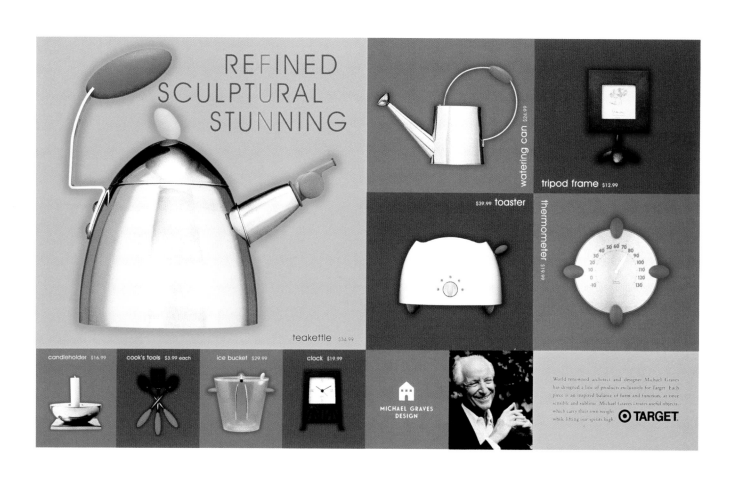

Agency: Design Guys Art Director: Steven Sikora Designer: Anne Peterson Photographer: Darrell Eager, Bill Phelps, Lars Hansen, Jim Erikson Copywriter: Jay Kaskel Client: Target Stores

STRAND BOOK STALL. GREAT BOOKS. GREAT PRICES.

STRAND BOOK STALL. GREAT BOOKS. GREAT PRICES.

'Dhannur', Sir PM Road, MUMBAI-1. Tel. 2661994, 2661719. Fax: 2088071. e/S-115 Manipal Centre, Dickenson Road, BANGALORE-42. Tel: 5580000. Fax: 5582222.

'Dhannur', Sir PM Road, MUMBAI-1. Tel. 2661994, 2661719. Fax: 2088071. e/S-115 Manipal Centre, Dickenson Road, BANGALORE-42. Tel: 5580000. Fax: 5582222.

STRAND BOOK STALL. GREAT BOOKS. GREAT PRICES.

STRAND BOOK STALL. GREAT BOOKS. GREAT PRICES.

'Dhannur', Sir PM Road, MUMBAI-1. Tel. 2661994, 2661719. Fax: 2088071. e/S-115 Manipal Centre, Dickenson Road, BANGALORE-42. Tel: 5580000. Fax: 5582222.

'Dhannur', Sir PM Road, MUMBAI-1. Tel. 2661994, 2661719. Fax: 2088071. e/S-115 Manipal Centre, Dickenson Road, BANGALORE-42. Tel: 5580000. Fax: 5582222.

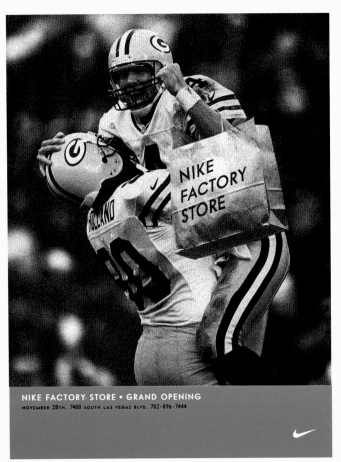

NIKE FACTORY STORE • GRAND OPENING
NOVEMBER 28TH. 7400 SOUTH LAS VEGAS BLVD. 702-896-7444

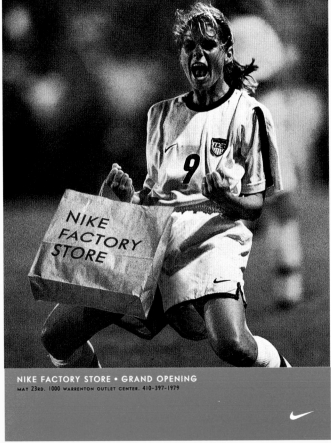

NIKE FACTORY STORE • GRAND OPENING
MAY 23RD. 1000 WARRENTON OUTLET CENTER. 410-397-1979

Agency: Goodby, Silverstein & Partners Art Director: Tyler Magnussen Creative Director: Rich Silverstein, Jeffrey Goodby Copywriter: Sharon Tao Client: Nike

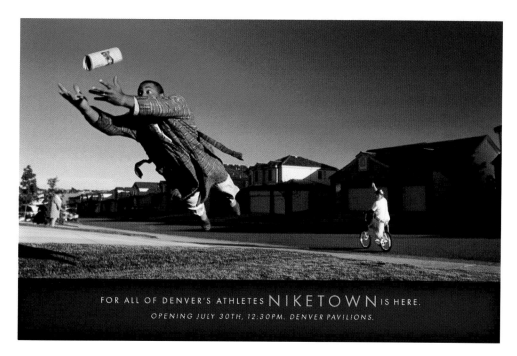

Agency: Goodby, Silverstein & Partners Art Director: Terry Finley Creative Director: Steve Simpson Photographer: Brad Harris Client: Nike

Agency: Fahlgren/Tampa Art Director: John Stapleton Creative Director: Scott Sheinberg Photographer: Brad Ausberger Copywriter: John Mims Client: Vertical Ventures

DEFY GRAVITY

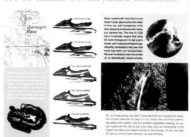

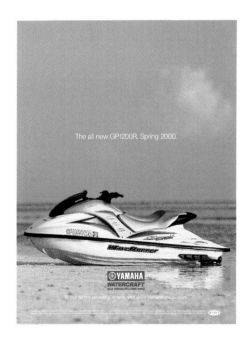

(top) Agency: Vitro Robertson Art Director: John Vitro Creative Director: John Robertson, John Vitro Designer: Doug Kress Photographer: Rob Brown Illustrator: Brad Palm Copywriter: Ben Whan Lee Client: Yamaha Motor Corp. *(bottom)* Agency: Vitro Roberts Art Director: Will Roth Creative Director: John Robertson, John Vitro Photographer: Rob Brown Copywriter: John Robertson Client: Yamaha Motor Corp.

According to the most
recent statistics on
cancer survival rates,
Lance Armstrong
is neither alive,
nor has he won the
Tour de France.

Just do it

www.laf.org

Agency: Goodby, Silverstein & Partners Art Director: Paul Hirsch Creative Director: Jeffrey Goodby, Rich Silverstein Photographer: Graham Watson Copywriter: Josh Denberg Client: Nike

Be careful.

Lorem ipsum dolor sit amet, consectetuer adipiscing elit, sed diam nonummy nibh euismod tincidunt ut laoreet dolore magna aliquam erat volutpat. Ut wisi enim ad minim veniam, quis nostrud exerci tation ullamcorper suscipit lobortis nisl ut aliquip ex ea commodo consequat. Duis autem vel eum iriure dolor in hendrerit in vulputate velit esse molestie consequat, vel illum dolore eu feugiat nulla facilisis at vero eros et accumsan et iusto odio dignissim qui blandit praesent luptatum zzril delenit augue duis dolore te feugait nulla facilisi. Lorem ipsum dolor sit amet, consectetuer adipiscing elit, sed diam nonummy nibh euismod tincidunt ut laoreet dolore magna aliquam erat volutpat. Ut wisi enim ad minim veniam, quis exerci tation ullamcorper suscipit lobortis nisl ut aliquip ex ea commodo consequat.

Duis autem vel eum iriure dolor in hendrerit in vulputate velit esse molestie consequat, vel illum dolore eu feugiat nulla facilisis at vero eros et accumsan et iusto odio dignissim qui blandit praesent luptatum zzril delenit augue duis dolore te feugait nulla facilisi. Nam liber tempor cum soluta nobis eleifend option congue nihil imperdiet doming id quod mazim placerat facer possim assum.

Lorem ipsum dolor sit amet, consectetuer adipiscing elit, sed diam nonummy nibh euismod tincidunt ut laoreet dolore magna aliquam erat volutpat. Ut wisi enim ad minim veniam, quis nostrud exerci tation ullamcorper suscipit lobortis nisl ut aliquip ex ea commodo consequat. Duis autem vel eum iriure dolor in hendrerit in vulputate velit esse molestie consequat, vel illum dolore eu nulla facilisis at.

consequat, vel illum dolore eu feugiat nulla facilisis at vero eros et accumsan et iusto odio dignissim qui blandit praesent luptatum zzril delenit augue duis dolore te feugait nulla facilisi. Lorem ipsum dolor sit amet, consectetuer adipiscing elit, sed diam nonummy nibh euismod tincidunt ut laoreet dolore magna aliquam erat volutpat.

Ut wisi enim ad minim veniam, quis nostrud exerci tation ullamcorper suscipit lobortis nisl ut aliquip ex ea commodo consequat. Duis autem vel eum iriure dolor in hendrerit in vulputate velit esse molestie consequat, vel illum dolore eu feugiat nulla facilisis. Lorem ipsum dolor sit amet, consectetuer adipiscing elit, sed diam nonummy nibh euismod tincidunt ut laoreet dolore magna aliquam erat volutpat.

Ut wisi enim ad minim veniam, quis nostrud exerci tation ullamcorper suscipit lobortis nisl ut aliquip ex ea commodo consequat. Duis autem vel eum iriure dolor in hendrerit in vulputate velit esse molestie consequat, vel illum dolore eu feugiat nulla facilisis at vero eros et accumsan et iusto odio dignissim qui blandit praesent luptatum zzril delenit augue duis dolore te feugait nulla facilisi.

Lorem ipsum dolor sit amet, consectetuer adipiscing elit, sed diam nonummy nibh euismod tincidunt ut laoreet dolore magna aliquam erat volutpat. Ut wisi enim ad minim veniam, quis nostrud exerci tation ullamcorper suscipit lobortis nisl ut aliquip ex ea commodo consequat. Duis autem vel eum iriure dolor in hendrerit in vulputate velit esse molestie consequat, vel

Vero eros et accumsan et iusto odio dignissim qui blandit praesent luptatum zzril delenit augue duis dolore te feugait nulla facilisi. Lorem ipsum dolor sit amet, consectetuer adipiscing elit, sed diam nonummy nibh euismod tincidunt ut laoreet dolore magna aliquam erat volutpat. Ut wisi enim ad minim veniam, quis nostrud exerci tation ullamcorper suscipit lobortis nisl ut aliquip ex ea commodo consequat.

Autem vel eum iriure dolor in hendrerit in vulputate velit esse molestie consequat, vel illum dolore eu feugiat nulla facilisis at vero eros et accumsan et iusto odio dignissim qui blandit praesent luptatum zzril delenit augue duis dolore te feugait nulla facilisi.

Lorem ipsum dolor sit amet, consectetuer adipiscing elit, sed diam nonummy nibh euismod tincidunt ut laoreet dolore magna aliquam erat volutpat. Ut wisi enim ad minim veniam, quis nostrud exerci tation ullamcorper suscipit lobortis nisl ut aliquip ex ea commodo consequat. Duis autem vel eum iriure dolor in hendrerit in vulputate velit esse molestie consequat, vel

Lorem ipsum dolor sit amet, consectetuer adipiscing elit, sed diam nonummy nibh euismod tincidunt ut laoreet dolore magna aliquam erat volutpat. Ut wisi enim ad minim veniam, quis nostrud exerci tation ullamcorper suscipit lobortis nisl ut aliquip ex ea commodo consequat. Duis autem vel eum iriure dolor in hendrerit in vulputate velit esse molestie consequat, vel illum dolore eu feugiat nulla facilisis at vero eros et accumsan et iusto odio dignissim qui blandit praesent luptatum zzril delenit augue duis dolore te feugait nulla facilisis.

Lorem ipsum dolor sit amet, consectetuer adipiscing elit, sed diam nonummy nibh euismod tincidunt ut laoreet dolore magna aliquam erat volutpat. Ut wisi enim ad minim veniam, quis nostrud exerci tation ullamcorper suscipit lobortis nisl ut aliquip ex ea commodo consequat. Duis autem vel eum iriure dolor in hendrerit in vulputate velit esse molestie consequat. Duis autem vel eum iriure dolor in hendrerit in vulputate velit esse molestie

consequat, vel illum dolore eu feugiat nulla facilisis at vero eros et accumsan et iusto odio dignissim qui blandit praesent luptatum zzril delenit augue duis dolore te feugait nulla facilisis.

It wisi enim ad minim veniam, quis nostrud exerci tation ullamcorper suscipit lobortis nisl ut aliquip ex ea commodo consequat. Duis autem vel eum iriure dolor in hendrerit in vulputate velit esse molestie consequat, vel illum dolore eu feugiat nulla facilisi.

Vero eros et accumsan et iusto odio dignissim qui blandit praesent luptatum zzril delenit augue duis dolore te feugait nulla facilisis. Lorem ipsum dolor sit amet, consectetuer adipiscing elit, sed diam nonummy nibh euismod tincidunt ut laoreet dolore magna aliquam erat volutpat.

Autem vel eum iriure dolor in hendrerit in vulputate velit esse molestie consequat, vel illum dolore eu feugiat nulla facilisis at vero eros et accumsan et iusto odio dignissim qui blandit praesent luptatum zzril delenit augue duis dolore te feugait nulla facilisi.

If you nail the fish
between the eyes,
it might spook him.

A rod so accurate, it's like an extension of your own arm. Or better yet, an extension of Jimmy Houston's arm.

SIGNATURE SERIES

SHIMANO

Duis autem vel eum iriure dolor in hendrerit in vulputate velit esse molestie consequat, vel

I N N O V A T E O R D I E

Hey numb-nuts, listen up.

Even if that mound of medical evidence didn't
exist, or that segment on 20/20 hadn't aired, or all those
doctors and specialists weren't concurring, even if all
you have to go on is the discomfort and numbness you
sometimes get riding a conventional saddle, isn't that enough
for you to consider the Body Geometry saddle? In a Stanford
University study, 24 out of 25 riders said the seat helped
relieve pressure on the sensitive perineal area, which,
as we all know, is a pretty important spot. Sure, the seat's
a little weird looking, but not nearly as weird as
what happens when that spot quits working.

I N N O V A T E O R D I E

Tough as nails? Oh come on,
you'll have to do better than that.

You'd have to want to pop an Armadillo tire. And
even then you probably can't. Thanks to our proprietary
casing and DuPont KEVLAR, Armadillos deflect incoming
particles and significantly prevent punctures and side
cuts, making them virtually indestructible. Centuries?
Double centuries? Try millenniums. One guy reports riding
four thousand miles on a set of Armadillos without a single flat.
Can this possibly be true? Well according to an independent
test, Armadillos are far and away the toughest tires out there.
And yet the smoothness of the ride is never compromised,
which is the whole point. Or points, as it were.

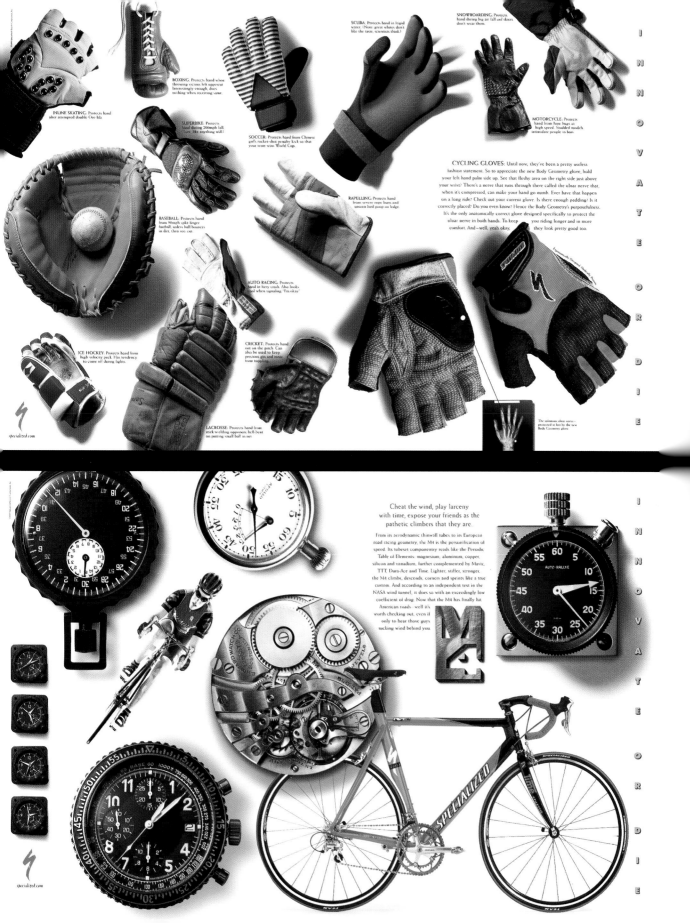

burgers and being a millionaire."

Standing over a six-foot putt can mess with your mind. But knowing that if you miss it, you miss your chance to qualify for the PGA Tour adds enough pressure to squeeze diamonds from a lump of coal.

ODYSSEY
Number one putter in golf

At the 1998 PGA Tour Qualifying Tournament, 19 of the 41 qualifiers – nearly 50% – chose to play with an Odyssey putter. The putter with the great-feeling Stronomic insert has been used by more players across the major tours these past three years than any other putter. Apparently when you're holding your life in your hands, you put a lot more thought into what putter you're holding.

Four years of getting people into a hole and then we discover our technology is just as good at getting you out of one.

From the minds that developed the number one putter in golf come gap, sand and lob wedges that bring a new level of feel to the short game. Our new Dual Force Wedges use an advanced material called Lyconite to dampen vibration and improve feel. Its light weight allows for better perimeter weighting. And since

ODYSSEY
Number one putter in golf

Lyconite is more durable than steel, the groove pattern won't wear down. So once you fall in love with them, they'll last forever. The short game has never felt so good.

If a putter dominates for one year, you can call it a "fluke."

If a putter dominates for two years, you can call it a "series of coincidences."

If a putter dominates for three years, what do you call it?

You call it, "my new putter."

(opposite top) Agency: Vitro Robertson Art Director: Will Roth Creative Director: John Robertson, John Vitro Designer: Peter Kramer Illustrator: Peter Kramer Copywriter: Dan Consiglio, John Robertson Client: Odyssey Golf (middle) Agency: Vitro Robertson Art Director: Will Roth Creative Director: John Robertson, John Vitro Designer: Peter Kramer Illustrator: Peter Kramer Copywriter: Brian Gold Client: Odyssey Golf (bottom) Agency: Vitro Robertson Art Director: Will Roth Creative Director: John Robertson, John Vitro Designer: Peter Kramer Illustrator: Peter Kramer Copywriter: Dan Consiglio, John Robertson Client: Odyssey Golf

Agency: Vitro Robertson Art Director: Kevin Kwan Creative Director: John Robertson, John Vitro Copywriter: John Robertson Client: Oakley

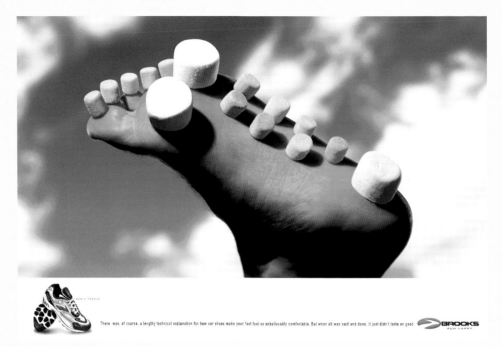

Agency: Big Bang Idea Engineering Art Director: Wade Koniakowsky Creative Director: Rob Bagot, Wade Koniakowsky Photographer: Mark Laita Copywriter: Rob Bagot Client: Brooks

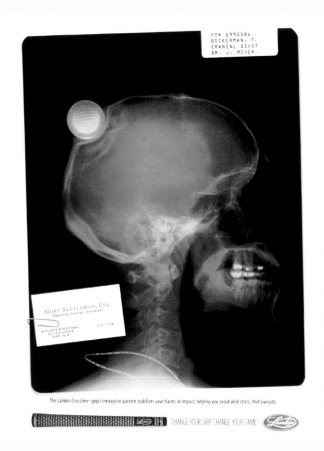

Agency: Matthews/Mark Art Director: Mark Albertazzi Creative Director: Michael Mark Photographer: Marshall Harrington Copywriter: Patrick Emerick Client: Lamkin Golf Grips

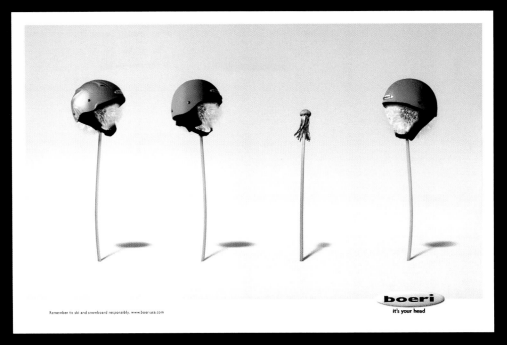

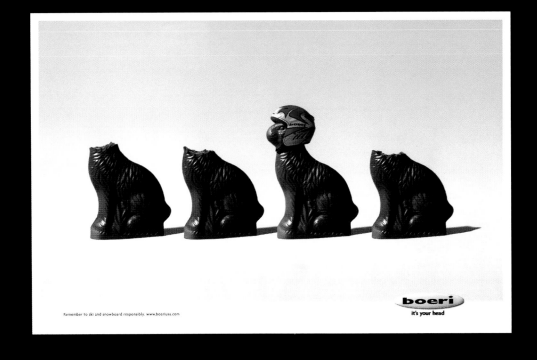

Agency: Mullen Art Director: Mary Rich Creative Director: Edward Boches, Greg Bokor Photographer: Craig Orsini Illustrator: Marc Ruggerio Copywriter: Stephen Mietelski Client: Boeri

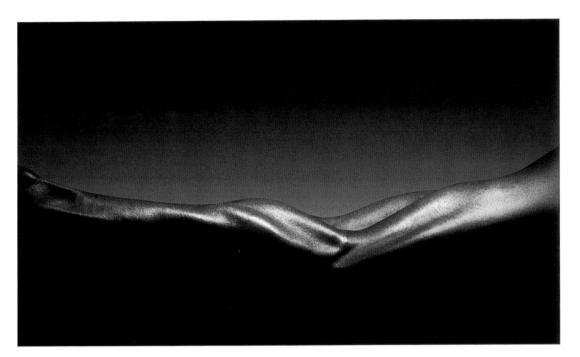

Pheasant Mountain Bikes

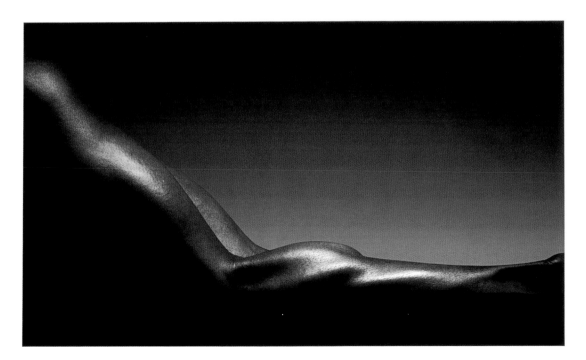

Pheasant Downhill Bikes

Agency: Goodby, Silverstein & Partners   Art Director: Paul Hirsch, Claude Shade, Josh Denberg Creative Director: Jeffrey Goodby, Rich Silverstein Photographer: Kenji Toma
Copywriter: Josh Denberg, Paul Hirsch Client: Nike

JULY, 15. THURS. Everywhere I see signs of people passing, but I rarely see the people themselves. They're hidden behind the glare of a car window, inside the silver skin of a distant airplane, or in the iron belly of a rumbling locomotive. Everyone seems to be encased in their own mobile world, constantly moving past and around each other, but never interacting. This isn't simply a result of the fact that everyone is confined in their own separate vehicle. It's more than that. Take my example - for the first hour or so the car but soon the sleepy sensation of constant sameness of the highway a hypnotic state. Within staring out the window Eventually this state be breaking, it seems not Talking in the car at this point stop then becomes like surfacing onto a little island of reality

HI-SPEED

Extensive traveling induces a feeling of encapsulation, and travel, so broadening at first, contracts the mind.

MADE IN U.S.A.

FILTERS

LUCKY STRIKE
CHARCOAL FILTER

LUCKIES
AN AMERICAN ORIGINAL

GO WITH LUCKY STRIKE

ency: Saatchi & Saatchi, Bates Yomiko   Art Director: Marcus Woolcott, Kiyotaka Kobayashi Creative Director: Marcus Woolcott Designer: Marcus Woolcott Photographer: Jeff Brown
rane Kazuyasu, Nakasuji Jun Copywriter: Marcus Woolcott Client: Brown & Williamson

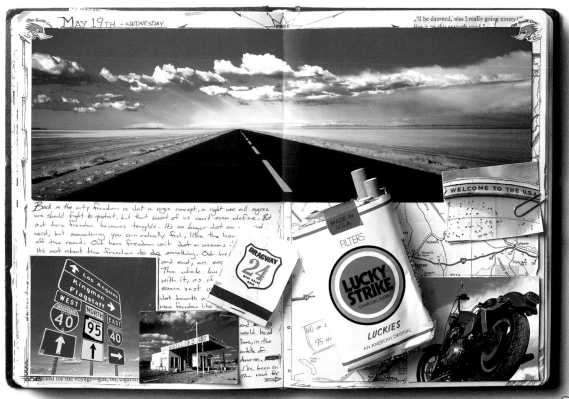

JUNE 21 - MONDAY

RANCH HOUSE
CAFE

STOP

★ LAST MINUTE AFFORDABLE TRAVEL ANYWHERE ★

t Check

Today, I called him from a pay phone in a cafe I&I ...well, but it sounds like its business as usual back

LUCKY STRIKE
CHARCOAL FILTER

MADE IN U.S.A.

FILTERS

LUCKIES
AN AMERICAN ORIGINAL

MAY 19TH - WEDNESDAY

"I'll be damned, was I really going ninety?"

Back in the city freedom is just a vague concept, a right we all agree we should fight to protect, but that most of us can't even define. But out here freedom becomes tangible. It's no longer just an ...ed word, but something you can actually feel, like the ...

WELCOME TO THE U.S.A

Los Angeles
Kingman
Flagstaff

WEST   NORTH   EAST
40   95   40

DRAGWAY
24

MADE IN U.S.A.

FILTERS

LUCKY STRIKE
CHARCOAL FILTER

LUCKIES
AN AMERICAN ORIGINAL

Agency: Gyro Art Director: Rosh Nort Creative Director: Steven Grasse Copywriter: Jerry the Nomad Photographer: Moshe Brakha Client: Camel

Beaver Creek VILLAGE
COLORADO

SKI·IN·LODGING·PERFORMING ARTS·BOUTIQUES·DINING

146 GROOMED TRAILS

VILLAGE TO VILLAGE SKIING
IN BEAVER CREEK®
C O L O R A D O

NORTH AMERICA'S GRAND MOUNTAIN RESORT™

NORTH AMERICA'S GRAND MOUNTAIN RESORT™

ALT. 11,440 FT.

WORLD CHAMPIONSHIP BIRDS OF PREY DOWNHILL

BEAVER CREEK

COLORADO

Agency: Fitzgerald & Co. Art Director: Karla Childers Creative Director: Jim Paddock Copywriter: Susan Willoughby Client: Aruba

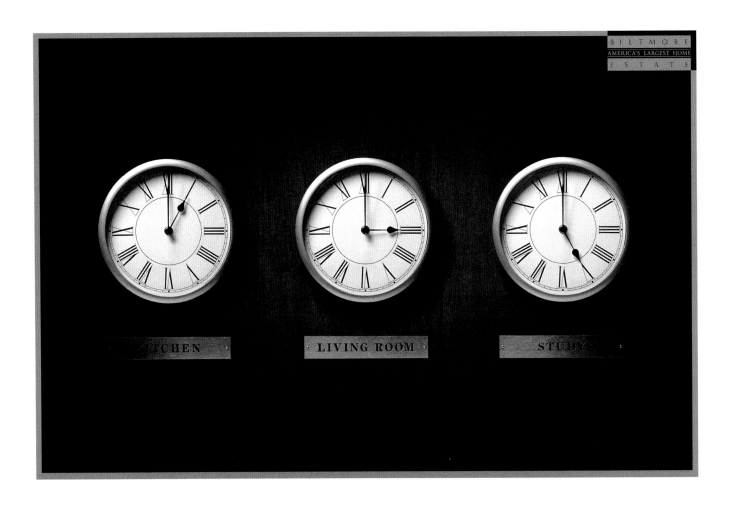

Agency: LKM Art Director: Doug Pedersen Creative Director: Jim Mountjoy Photographer: Jim Arndt Copywriter: Curtis Smith Client: Biltmore

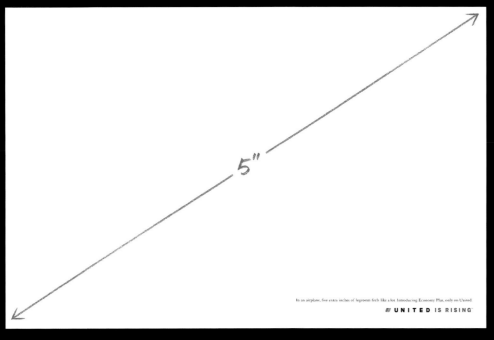

(top) Agency: Fallon McElligott Art Director: Dan Bryant Creative Director: David Lubars Copywriter: Scott Cooney Client: United *(middle)* Agency: Fallon McElligott Art Director: Tom Lichtenheld Creative Director: David Lubars Illustrator: Tom Lichtenheld Copywriter: Tom Rosen Client: United *(bottom)* Agency: Fallon McElligott Art Director: Dan Bryant Creative Director: David Lubars Copywriter: Scott Cooney Client: United

NATIVE BIRDS of NORTH CAROLINA

Purple Martin
(Progne subis)
Coloration: Blue-black above and below.
Range: Southern Canada to South America.
Habitat: Towns, farms, open country, often near water.
Song: Gurgling.

Blue Grosbeak
(Guiraca caerulea)
Coloration: Blue with two tan wing bars.
Range: Central US to Central America.
Habitat: Brush, streamside thickets.
Song: Rapid warble.

Cardinal
(Cardinalis cardinalis)
Coloration: All-red body with pointed crest, black patch at base of bill.
Range: Southern Ontario to Central America.
Habitat: Woodlands, thickets, gardens, towns.
Song: Clear, slurred whistle.

Pileated Woodpecker
(Dryocopus pileatus)
Coloration: Black with flaming red crest.
Range: Canada to southern US.
Habitat: Conifer, hardwood and mixed forests.
Song: Loud, ringing call.

Carolina Wren
(Thryothorus ludovicianus)
Coloration: Warm reddish brown above, buff below. White eyebrow stripe.
Range: Eastern US and Mexico.
Habitat: Tangles, brush, suburban gardens, towns.
Song: 3-syllabled chant.

Short-Eared Owl
(Asio flammeus)
Coloration: Streaked tawny brown with dark face disks and yellow eyes.
Range: Nearly worldwide.
Habitat: Prairies, marshes, dunes, tundra.
Song: Sneezy bark.

Belted Kingfisher
(Megaceryle alcyon)
Coloration: Blue-gray above with ragged, bushy crest and broad gray breastband.
Range: Alaska to southern US and Central America.
Habitat: Streams, lakes, bays, coasts; nests in banks.
Song: Loud, dry rattle.

Fulvous Whistling Duck
(Dendrocygna bicolor)
Coloration: Tawny body, dark back, pale side stripe. White ring on rump.
Range: Southern US to South America.
Habitat: Mainly coastal marshes.
Song: Squealing, slurred whistle.

Carolina Chickadee
(Parus carolinensis)
Coloration: Black cap and bib, white cheeks.
Range: Southern New Jersey to Gulf Coast.
Habitat: Mixed and deciduous woods; willow thickets, groves, shade trees.
Song: 4-syllabled whistle.

Eastern Bluebird
(Sialia sialis)
Coloration: Blue body with rusty red breast.
Range: Southern Canada to Central America.
Habitat: Open country with scattered trees; farms, roadsides.
Song: 3 or 4 soft gurgling notes.

Midway Airlines CRJ
(Aerius carolinensis)
Coloration: White body, yellow tail with blue markings.
Range: East of Rockies to Eastern seaboard.
Habitat: Airports; nests in Raleigh/Durham.
Song: Low roar.

With more than 190 flights a day departing to destinations ranging from Boston, MA to Ft. Lauderdale, FL and all points in between, there's no better way to take flight from Raleigh/Durham. 1-800-44-MIDWAY

Midway AIRLINES   www.midwayair.com

Agency: LKM Art Director: Doug Pedersen Creative Director: Jim Mountjoy Illustrator: Jon Steele, David Wilgus Copywriter: Curtis Smith Client: Midway

Learn from the experts.

For complete vacation packages to Alaska, call your travel agent
or Alaska Airlines Vacations for details. 1.800.468.2248

Complete vacation packages
to Palm Springs.

Call your travel agent or Alaska Airlines Vacations for details.
1.800.468.2248

(top) Agency: Wongdoody Art Director: Jason Black Creative Director: Tracy Wong Photographer: Randy Allbritton Copywriter: Dean Saling Client: Alaska Airlines *(bottom)*
Agency: Wongdoody Art Director: Jason Black Creative Director: Tracy Wong Photographer: Randy Allbritton Copywriter: Jacket McCullough Client: Alaska Airlines

FERDINAND
MAGELLAN
PONCE
DE LEON
STAN
FROM BALTIMORE

Welcome to your National Forest.
Set out with your skis or your board and explore the vast and remote world that is Keystone. Trail maps are available for the slightly less adventurous. Condos start at $110 per night. For more information call 800.660.5146. The Nature of the Rockies.

 KEYSTONE

ENCHANTED
FORESTS,
WICKED
DOUBLE DIAMONDS.

Welcome to your National Forest.
Three mountains, back to back to back, lead you deep into Nature's playground—where the loudest sound you'll hear is the beating of your heart. Condos start at $110 per night. For more information, please call 888.239.3717. The Nature of the Rockies.

 KEYSTONE

Prime Minister of Faraway "Explore." It is the one-word philosophy of the Floating Utopian Society of Crystal Cruises, as summarized by its Prime Minister and Captain. We are creating a more perfect society, in which everything wonderful is possible, elegance and friendliness are inalienable rights, and a great colorful curious world rises up to meet you. When you sail aboard Crystal Cruises, you will agree: *It's a* WONDERFUL world.

CRYSTAL CRUISES

Ministry of Tasty Bits In the Floating Utopian Society of Crystal Cruises, even the tiniest tart is an urgent matter of state. Because, in our ideal world, every detail matters and everything wonderful is possible. (The tart above, strawberry-rhubarb, was baked off the China coast, the rhubarb obtained in Shanghai, simply because a guest fancied it.) When you sail aboard Crystal Cruises, you will agree: *It's a* WONDERFUL world.

CRYSTAL CRUISES

Ministry of Eccentric Requests In our Floating Utopian Society, few services are beyond us. For one guest, we flew in a case of *Corton-Charlemagne*; for another, a basketball hoop. We even grew wheatgrass on board, for someone's morning shake. Yet the most common request is for teddy bears—because there's always a child back home, who always approves. Sail with Crystal Cruises, and you'll agree: *It's a* WONDERFUL world.

CRYSTAL CRUISES

Ministry of Sniff In the Floating Utopian Society of Crystal Cruises, our sommeliers and cellar-masters preside over the finest and most extensive wine cellar at sea—and they can sniff out a Château Pétrus at a hundred paces. (What good is a Utopia, if you can't get a Pétrus there?) On board Crystal, everything good in the world is ready to be served. When you sail with Crystal Cruises, you will agree: *It's a* WONDERFUL world.

CRYSTAL CRUISES

(top) Agency: Goodby, Silverstein & Partners Art Director: Claude Shade Creative Director: Steve Simpson, Rich Silverstein Photographer: Guzman Photography Illustrator: Wes Hardison Copywriter: Steve Simpson Client: Crystal Cruises *(bottom)* Agency: Goodby, Silverstein & Partners Art Director: Claude Shade Creative Director: Steve Simpson, Rich Silverstein Photographer: Fabrizio Gianni Illustrator: Wes Hardison Copywriter: Steve Simpson Client: Crystal Cruises

Southwest Airlines. Proud Sponsor Of The Portland Rose Festival.

©1999 Southwest Airlines Co.

Agency: GSD&M Art Director: Steve Newton Creative Director: Brian Brooker Photographer: Dennis Fagan Copywriter: Mark Ray Client: Southwest Airlines

Index

PhotographersIllustratorsCopywriters

Agencies Clients

CreativeDirectorsArtDirectorsDesigners

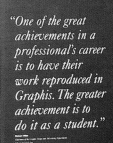

Design Annual 2000

Photo Annual 2000

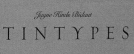

TINTYPES

Jayne Hinds Bidaut

Kazumasa Nagai
Geof Kern
Del Terrelonge
Gavino Sanna
Cahan & Associates
Matthew Carter

GRAPHIS $32.5

GRAPHIS
DesignAgencies.Com

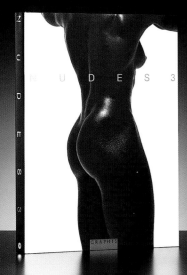

NUDES 3

GRAPHIS

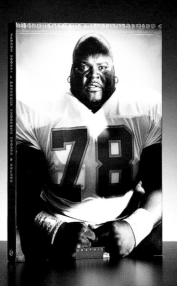

GRAPHIS

Advertising Annual 2000

Order Form

We're introducing a great way to reward *Graphis* magazine readers: If you subscribe to *Graphis*, you'll qualify for a 40% discount on our books. If you subscribe and place a Standing Order, you'll get a 50% discount on our books. A Standing Order means we'll reserve your selected Graphis Annual or Series title(s) at press and ship it to you at 50% discount. With a Standing Order for *Design Annual 2001*, for example, you'll receive this title at half-off, and each coming year, we'll send you the newest *Design Annual* at this low price—an ideal way for the professional to keep informed, year after year. In addition to the titles here, we carry books in all communication disciplines, so call if there's another title we can get for you. Thank you for supporting Graphis.

Book title	Order No.	Retail	40% off Discount	Standing Order 50% off	Quantity	Totals	Call for Entries
Advertising Annual 1999	1500	☐ $70.00	☐ $42.00	☐ $35.00			
Advertising Annual 2000	1550	☐ $70.00	☐ $42.00	☐ $35.00			
Advertising's Top Ten	195x	☐ $70.00	☐ $42.00	N/A			
African Journey	1992	☐ $70.00	☐ $42.00	N/A			
Annual Report 7	1895	☐ $70.00	☐ $42.00	☐ $35.00			
Apple Design	1259	☐ $45.00	☐ $27.00	N/A			
Black & White Blues	4710	☐ $40.00	☐ $24.00	N/A			
Book Design 2 (s)	1453	☐ $70.00	☐ $42.00	☐ $35.00			
Brochures 3 (s)	1496	☐ $70.00	☐ $42.00	☐ $35.00			
Corporate Identity 3 (s)	1437	☐ $70.00	☐ $42.00	☐ $35.00			
Design Annual 2001	1887	☐ $70.00	☐ $42.00	☐ $35.00			
Ferenc Berko	1445	☐ $60.00	☐ $36.00	N/A			
Graphic Art of Michael Schwab	1968	☐ $60.00	☐ $36.00	N/A			
Interactive Design 1 (s)	1631	☐ $70.00	☐ $42.00	☐ $35.00			
New Talent Design Annual 1999	1607	☐ $60.00	☐ $36.00	☐ $30.00			
New Talent Design Annual 2000	1640	☐ $60.00	☐ $36.00	☐ $30.00			
Nudes 1	212	☐ $50.00	☐ $30.00	N/A			
Photo Annual 1998	1461	☐ $70.00	☐ $42.00	☐ $35.00			
Product Design 2 (s)	1330	☐ $70.00	☐ $42.00	☐ $35.00			
Tintypes	1798	☐ $60.00	☐ $36.00	N/A			
T-Shirt Design 2 (s)	1402	☐ $60.00	☐ $36.00	☐ $30.00			
Walter Iooss	1569	☐ $60.00	☐ $36.00	N/A			
World Trademarks	1070	☐ $250.00	☐ $150.00	N/A			

Shipping & handling per book, US $7.00, Canada $15.00 USD, International $20.00 USD.		N/A
New York State shipments add 8.25% tax. All figures are in US dollars.		N/A

Standing Orders I understand I am committing to the selected annuals and/or series and will be automatically charged for each new volume in forthcoming years, at 50% off. I must call and cancel my order when I am no longer interested in purchasing the book. (To honor your Standing Order discount you must sign below.)

Signature _____ Date _____

Calls For Entry
If you would like to receive a call for entry for any of the annuals or series please check the appropriate box, in the last column above. You can also find contest information on the Graphis website:

www.graphis.com

Graphis magazine				
	☐ One year subscription	USA $90	Canada $125	Int'l $125
	☐ Two year subscription	USA $165	Canada $235	Int'l $235
	☐ One year student*	USA $65	Canada $90	Int'l $90
	☐ Single or Back Issues (per)	USA $24	Canada $28	Int'l $28

*All students must mail a copy of student ID along with the order form.
(s) = series (published every 2-4 years)

AA 2000

Name	☐ American Express ☐ Visa ☐ Mastercard ☐ Check
Company	
Address	Card #
City State Zip	Expiration
Daytime phone	Card holder's signature

Send this order form (or copy) and make check payable to Graphis Inc. For even faster turn-around service, or if you have any questions about subscribing, contact us at the following numbers: in the US (800) 209.4234; outside the US (212) 532. 9387 ext. 242 or 240; fax (212) 696.4242. Check for our mailing address or order Graphis anywhere in the world at www.graphis.com.

Graphis Books **Call For Entry**

If you would like us to put you on our mailing lists for Call for Entries for any of our books, please fill out the form and check off the specific books you would like to be a part of. We are now consolidating our mailings twice a year for our spring and fall books. If information is needed on specific deadlines for any of our books, please consult our web site: www.graphis.com.

Graphic Design Books		**Photography Books**	**Student Books**
☐ Advertising Annual	☐ Poster Annual	☐ Digital Photo (Professional)	☐ Advertising Annual
☐ Annual Reports	☐ Products by Design	☐ Human Con. (Photojournalism)	☐ Design Annual
☐ Book Design	☐ Letterhead	☐ New Talent (Amateur)	☐ Photo Annual (Professional)
☐ Brochure	☐ Logo Design	☐ Nudes (Professional)	☐ Products by Design
☐ Corporate Identity	☐ Music CD	☐ Nudes (Fine Art)	**All the Books**
☐ Design Annual	☐ New Media	☐ Photo Annual (Professional)	☐ All Design Books only
☐ Digital Fonts	☐ Packaging	☐ Photography (Fine Art)	☐ All Photo Books only
☐ Diagrams	☐ Paper Promotions		☐ All Students Books only
	☐ Typography		

First Name: _____ Last Name: _____

Company: _____

Telephone: _____ Fax: _____

Mailing Address: _____ City: _____

State, Country: _____ Zip: _____

Mail or fax form to: Graphis, Call for Entries, 307 Fifth Ave., Tenth Floor, New York, New York 10016, USA, or fax to 212.213.3229

Order Graphis on the Web from anywhere in the world: **www.graphis.com**